ALL-STAR

ACTIVITY BOOK

LIBERTY
STREET

Writer: James Buckley, Jr.
Executive Editor: Beth Sutinis
Art Director: Georgia Morrissey
Designer: Penny Lamprell
Production Manager: Hillary Leary
Prepress Manager: Alex Voznesenskiy

Special thanks to the Sports Illustrated Kids team: Mark Bechtel and Beth Bugler

ISBN: 978-1-68330-773-0

First Edition, 2017
1 QGS 17
1 3 5 7 9 8 6 4 2

We welcome your comments and
suggestions about Time Inc. Books.
Please write to us at:

Time Inc. Books
Attention: Book Editors
P.O. Box 62310
Tampa, FL 33662-2310
(800) 765-6400

timeincbooks.com

Time Inc. Books products may be purchased for business or promotional use. For information on bulk purchases, please contact Christi Crowley in the Special Sales Department at (845) 895-9858.

Contents

Baseball

Take us out to the ball game, take us out with the crowd! Put down your peanuts and pick up a pencil to take on these hardball challenges. Stare down the pitcher and hit a homer!

Hall of Fame

BABE RUTH

TED WILLIAMS

MICKEY MANTLE

BOB GIBSON

GREG MADDUX

KEN GRIFFEY JR.

BASEBALL BY THE NUMBERS!

Combine your insider knowledge of baseball with a little bit of number magic. Translate the words into numbers and do the math to get the answers!

Example: Number of bases in a double x number of players in a batting order = 2 x 9 = 18

 1 Number of RBI on a grand slam + number of bases in a double − number of base coaches = _____ + _____ − _____ = _____

 2 Number of Major League teams − (number of bases in a home run x number of bases in a single) = _____ − (_____ x _____) = _____

 3 Number of balls in a walk x number of umpires in a regular-season game = _____ x _____ = _____

 4 Number of outfielders x number of outs in a full inning − number of bases in a triple = _____ x _____ − _____ = _____

5 Number of strikes needed for a strikeout x (number of outs in a half inning + number of innings in a game) = _____ x (_____ + _____) = _____

Andrew McCutchen

Pro Tip

Want to know your batting average? Divide the number of hits you got by the number of official at-bats you had (remember, don't include walks or hit-by-pitches or sacrifices as at-bats). For example, if Pirates All-Star Andrew McCutchen had 80 hits in 240 at-bats, his average would be 80 divided by 240, or .333. That's all-star level!

BASEBALL WORD SEARCH

Here's a puzzle to work on between innings. Find the names of 20 MLB All-Stars. Look up, down, and even diagonally to fill up your superstar roster!

```
                    R F E
                F I O G R I F E F
            W X I O T C U E E O J E L
        S D A F G D H M Z U B Q W T S M P
        Q Y O R B K Y M B O R N E D L L F F O
      G C H K F A V F X A R E G A E S E G F F N
      V V P W X P A G M A N M E Z I Z M R N A W
    D B O R M R F S G O Z E S V P S W A E A P Q C
    Z M K U G O L B L R E H O E S O D H N L X T Q
  Q I B Q M E C Q R W C E B H F A C B J R D W A I S
  F I Z D K Q Y Z W Q B N D Y C L K Q D A C B H Y I
  I E A F H F S J G Q M P C N V E Y I M G D N S N P
S O A U K B N C I O Y C N S S Y Y A Y V M T P W G L C
C K M W Q C R C J L T L P T L G S D E O U P R Z F N M
L D I V O P Y B H D L O T R R H T S S H B W Q C I R V
  I L X Y M K X E S K E D R V I U G O J A T T A B V
  B B W R P V P T C B I D S M S O E P S X R H B B O
  K Y Y W G Q T A H S Z T A P K R V S C Z T P R F K
    Y W L Q Q O N M Z P L J B L T U A T X B I E L
    I W C Y D U P I N K Y H J R G T G K F L F R R
    N E S N A J D R Z I Y U N J L N E O V G A
      R H I B B L T C N I M A C H A D O J H H O
      L I I E H T D U B G B B B K W P Y L G G
        X V R V R N O E L D R I P O W Q F
        N D G M A Y T O J E Q R Y
          A V S U C O M D L
            T F N
```

Hosmer	**Trout**	**Hamels**	**Harper**	**Jansen**
Altuve	**Cabrera**	**Sale**	**Murphy**	**Syndergaard**
Machado	**Trumbo**	**Posey**	**Seager**	**Cueto**
Betts	**Kimbrel**	**Fowler**	**Bumgarner**	**Goldschmidt**

CAP IT OFF!

These seven MLB All-Stars ran out to the field, but they grabbed the wrong hats! Can you draw lines showing which hat each player should be wearing?

All-Star Fact

Have you ever worn a rally cap? If you play or watch baseball, you know that when your team is behind late in the game, it's time for a rally. To bring good luck, wear your cap inside out, or backward, or in a silly shape. Does it work? Well, sure . . . sometimes it does!

KRIS BRYANT
Chicago Cubs

BUSY DAY AT THE BALLPARK!

Kris Bryant is one serious slugger. But he has to do his job at loud and crazy Wrigley Field. Here's Bryant at bat at Wrigley. Check out the list of things below and see if you can find all of them in the picture. Bryant can't look, of course—he's waiting for a fastball to send into next week!

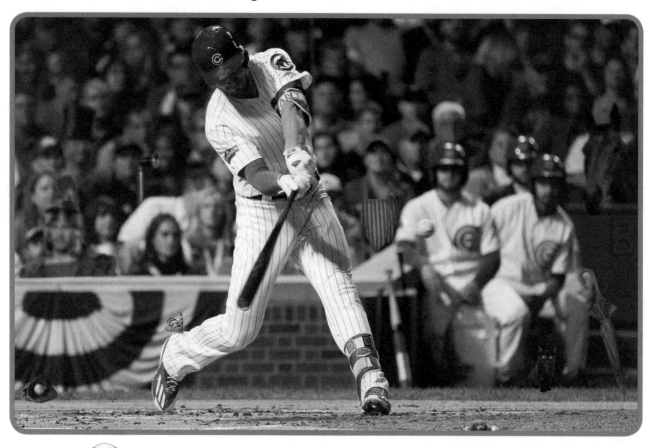

Find and circle these things in the picture.

umbrella	butterfly	horse
Cubs logo	periscope	cook's apron
catcher's mitt	mole	top hat
fan in green hat	letter B	striped bat
kitten	2 baseballs	gladiator

MEMORY CARD

All-Star Fact

Look carefully at this image for two minutes. Have a friend time you, or use an app (or, you know, a clock!). Look at the names, faces, and other details. Then cover the picture with a piece of paper and see how many questions you can answer without peeking!

The most valuable baseball card ever sold was a 1909 card featuring Honus Wagner. There was no All-Star Game when he played, but if there had been, he would have made it every year! Wagner was among the first five players inducted into the Baseball Hall of Fame, in 1936.

1. What team did Cecil Fielder play for?
2. In how many pictures is Don Mattingly wearing a glove?
3. What is "McGee's" first name?
4. True or false: There are pictures of Mattingly with AND without a mustache.
5. Did Wade Boggs hit left-handed or right-handed?

Collect them all!

Your Little League team is having its end-of-season celebration. Bring your colored pencils or markers and create trading cards for a few of your favorite Major Leaguers. By the way, you can design your own baseball card and put yourself in your favorite player's uniform. You might end up in Cooperstown at the Hall of Fame someday!

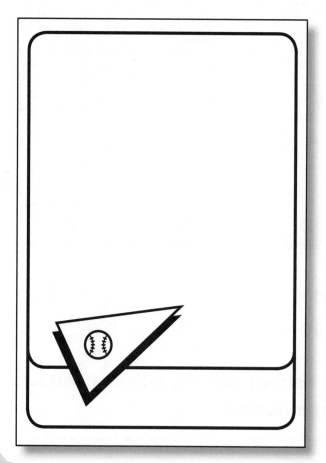

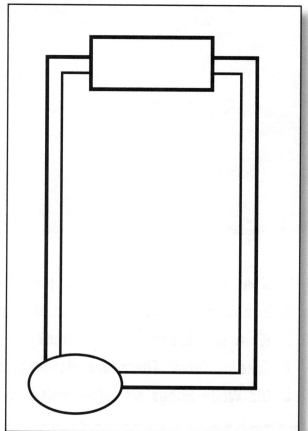

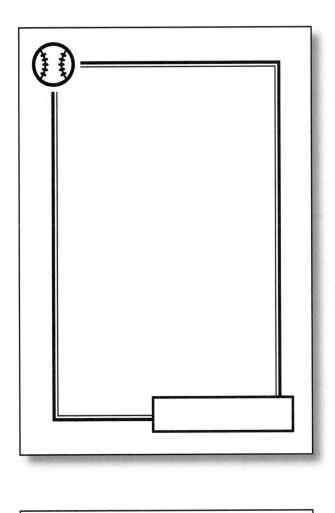

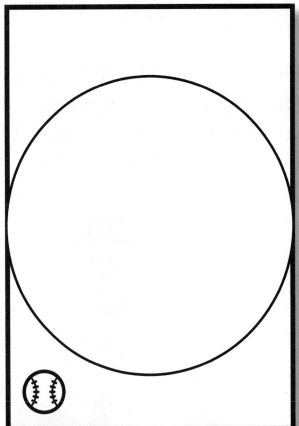

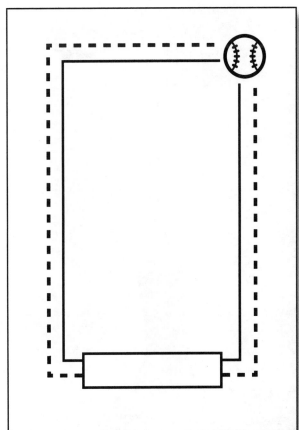

YOU CAN'T PLAY LIKE THAT!

Pirates star Andrew McCutchen was in a hurry when he got dressed for today's game. Can you help him out and circle all the things that are wrong with his look? Hurry! There are eight things to find, and the Pirates need their All-Star in the lineup!

1

2

3

4

5

6

7

8

All-Star Fact

Baseball is the only sport that requires managers to dress like players. Managers have to be in uniform if they want to go on the field to change pitchers or talk with umpires. Good thing they don't do that in basketball—some coaches just would not look good in shorts.

BASEBALL BASE-ICS CROSSWORD

Use the clues to fill in the grid and show off your ball skills!

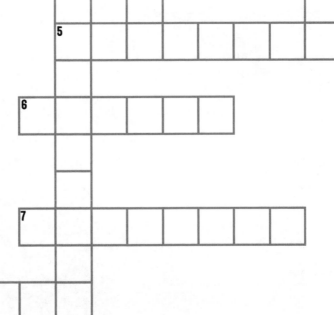

Across

2. A spherical object you can't play without, OR a pitch outside the strike zone

5. Left, center, and right are positions here

6. You can't bat without this on your head

7. The fence or net behind the catcher that keeps fans safe from foul balls

8. First, second, or third _____

Down

1. A nickname for a ball field

3. The special name for a catcher's glove

4. The only base that is shaped like a pentagon (two words)

MIXED-UP MASCOTS

Big confusion in the baseball mascot locker room! All the nameplates fell off the lockers. It's up to you to match them up. Draw a line connecting each mascot name with the team it cheers for.
And pay attention: a couple of fake mascot names snuck in there!

Phillies Cardinals Nationals Red Sox Mets Marlins

Phanatic

Screech

Bernie

Mr. Met

Wally the Green Monster

Sluggerrr

Bubbles

The left-field wall at Fenway Park is known as the Green Monster. It stands more than 37 feet tall. Fans can now sit atop the wall in "Monster seats."

Mariners **Astros** **Royals** **Orioles** **Brewers** **Athletics**

Jay Jay

Beanball

Stomper

Billy

The Bird

Fredbird

Orbit

Moose

MIXING UP HIS PITCHES

The sports network editor needs your help! She wants to run this footage of Zack Wheeler of the New York Mets throwing a game-winning strike, but the digital images got scrambled in the software. Help her out by reordering the images 1 to 6 to make the sequence make sense.

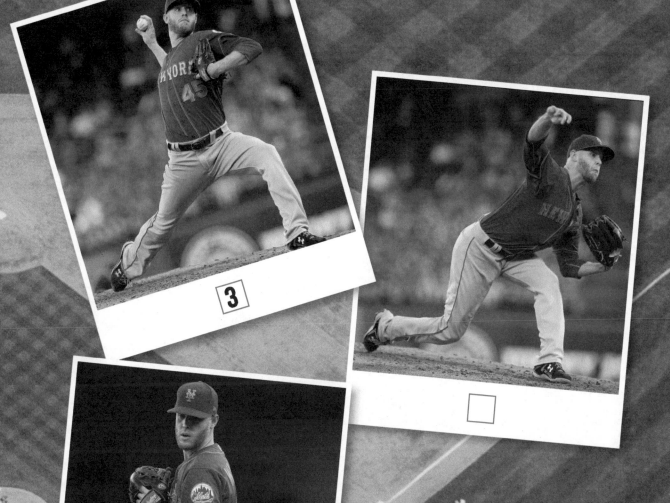

3

What has 18 legs and catches flies?

A baseball team.

Tell me a joke!

Football

Hut, hut, hike! Can you find all the answers and reach the end zone of these football puzzles? Put on your thinking helmet and score. The crowd goes wild!

Hall of Fame

JIM THORPE

RED GRANGE

OTTO GRAHAM

JOE MONTANA

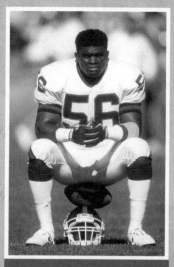

LAWRENCE TAYLOR

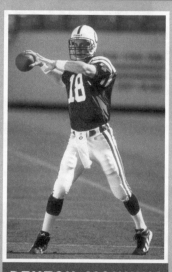

PEYTON MANNING

GRIDIRON GRID!

Answer the clues and fill in the grid to earn your championship ring!

Across

4. A placekick worth three points
5. The NFL's championship game
6. A quarterback moves the ball by handing it off, running with it, or _____ it
10. Where touchdowns are scored
11. The player who snaps the ball

Down

1. When a ballcarrier drops the ball
2. An interception returned for a touchdown
3. A defensive player who plays between the line of scrimmage and the backs
7. The name of a position on the line, OR the act of stopping a ballcarrier
8. He boots the ball high and deep on fourth down
9. This protects a player's head

FIX THE FIELD!

It's almost time for the Super Bowl. The field crew needs your help getting set up. Draw the items in the storage shed in their correct places on the field. Can you get everything in place in time for the coin flip?

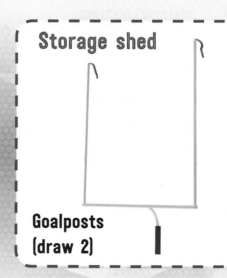

Storage shed

Goalposts (draw 2)

END ZONE

◄10 ◄20 ◄30 ◄40

◄OT ◄OS ◄OƐ ◄Oⴑ

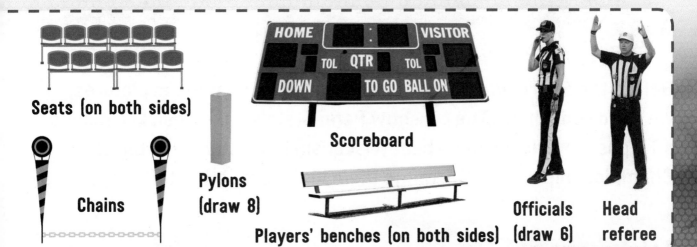

Seats (on both sides)

Chains

Pylons (draw 8)

Scoreboard

Players' benches (on both sides)

Officials (draw 6)

Head referee

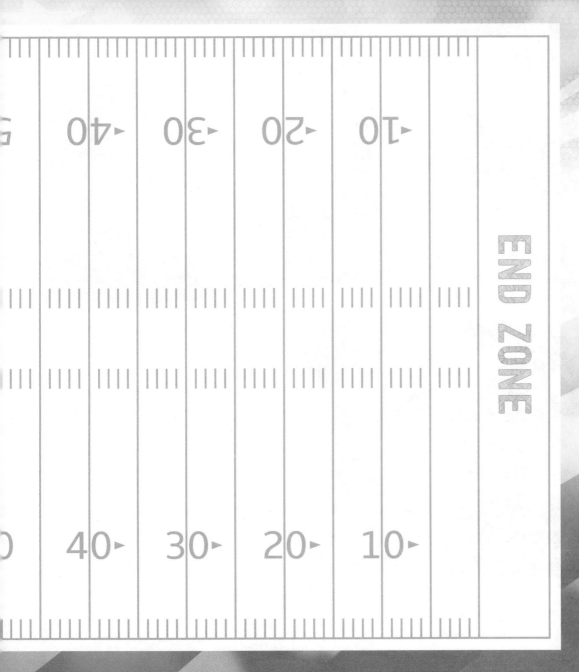

40 ► 30 ► 20 ► 10 ►

END ZONE

40 ► 30 ► 20 ► 10 ►

NO, YOU'RE OUT OF ORDER!

Before the *Sports Illustrated Kids* website can post these pictures, we need some help. The pix show Penn State's Mike Gesicki catching a TD pass to help his team beat Wisconsin to win the 2016 Big Ten Championship. Can you arrange them in the order that they happened?

1

Uniform makeover

NFL teams often experiment with different uniform designs. Each team has special jerseys that celebrate its team history, for example. For some Thursday games, teams wear solid colors, from shoes to helmets. Here's your chance

All-Star Fact

The first NFL team to have a logo painted on its helmet was the Rams. Former running back Fred Gehrke painted horns on the team's leather helmets in 1948. He was paid $1 per helmet to paint 75 helmets.

Jared Goff

to get creative. Grab your markers or crayons and use these drawings of NFL star Aaron Rodgers to give his uniform a new look. Will you change the colors? Add patterns? What about accessories? There are no rules—just a chance for you to make NFL fashion history!

AARON RODGERS
Green Bay Packers

TOM TERRIFIC!

Tom Brady has won more Super Bowl championships than any other quarterback in NFL history. He loves his trophies so much that he carries them around with him all the time. Can you look carefully at this photo of Brady and find six Vince Lombardi Trophies hidden in the art?

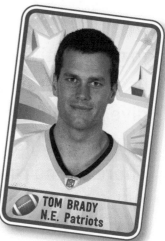

TOM BRADY
N.E. Patriots

| 1 | 2 | 3 | 4 | 5 | 6 |

All-Star Fact

The Super Bowl trophy was renamed after the great Vince Lombardi not long after his death in 1970. Lombardi led the Packers to five NFL championships in the 1960s, including victories in Super Bowls I and II.

NFL CRISSCROSS

The names of the NFL players on the roster fit into the grid below. Can you figure out how they should go? (Here's a hint: See which names start with the same letter. A couple of head-start letters are filled in for you.) Each player's last name will be used just once.

ODELL BECKHAM
N.Y. Giants

Roster

7 letters
Odell BECKHAM
Emmanuel SANDERS

6 letters
Melvin GORDON
Andy DALTON
T.Y. HILTON

5 letters
Antonio BROWN
Tom BRADY
Travis KELCE
Alex SMITH

4 letters
Derek CARR
Matt RYAN

PRO BOWL CONFUSION!

Someone has hacked the NFL Pro Bowl website. The names of all the players are mixed up. It's time for you to take action. Using your knowledge of the NFL, unscramble each Pro Bowl player's name. Here's the tricky part: one extra letter has snuck into each last name. After you figure out which letters are out of place, see if you can make a football word out of them!

1 LIJUO JOEOSN

2 ILHAKL ACKMC

3 TAMT NARYD

4 TMO BAOYRD

5 RANOA DDALONN

6 ONV IMWELLR

7 JSUTNI REKCUTH

8 TSIVAR LEUKCE

9 ZEEKEIL LLITOTET

1 ——— ———— ————

2 ———— ———— —

3 ———— ————

4 ——— ————

5 ———— —————

6 ——— —————

7 ———— —————

8 ———— ————

9 ———————— —————

Spare letters:

——————————

Answer:

☐☐☐☐☐☐☐☐☐

What do you need to eat super cereal?

Tell me a joke!

A Super Bowl!

BONUS How many three-letter words can you find in **Panthers** without scrambling the letters around? We found four!

STAR WITH WORDS

The names of some NFL superstars have shorter words hidden inside them. Can you take some of the short words in the word bank and use them to finish the last names of nine Pro Bowl heroes?

Word Bank
ROW
MILL
WAG
ROD
JAY
HAM
TON
CAMP
HAY

_ _ _ _ _NER

_ _ _ _ _ _BELL

B_ _ _ _N

_ _ _ _WARD

Pro Tip

Don't scramble the letters in the word bank words!

_ _ _ GERS

HIL_ _ _ _ _

BECK_ _ _ _

A_ _ _ _I

_ _ _ _ _ _ER

29

Super Bowl Party!

This year, you are hosting your first Super Bowl party with your friends. But first you need a menu. Guacamole, soda, nachos, chips, pizza, wings! Color your favorite football foods below and you'll be sure to score a touchdown with your family and friends.

 # Basketball

The clock is ticking down—time for one last puzzle. The outlet pass goes to you. The fans are going wild! You check your answers, fill in the last box, and the buzzer goes off! Did you win?

Hall of Fame

OSCAR ROBERTSON

BILL RUSSELL

LARRY BIRD

MAGIC JOHNSON

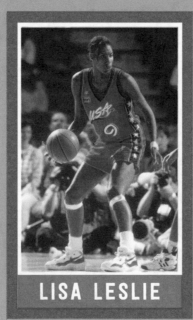

LISA LESLIE

MICHAEL JORDAN

NBA WORD SEARCH

NBA fans are always searching for their favorite players. They look for them online and they track them down in arenas. They follow them on Twitter and they check YouTube for the latest clips. Here's your chance to search for NBA stars, too! Find the last names of these 15 NBA superstuds and circle them. Like they do on the court, the players might be going backward, sideways, or up and down!

Steph Curry

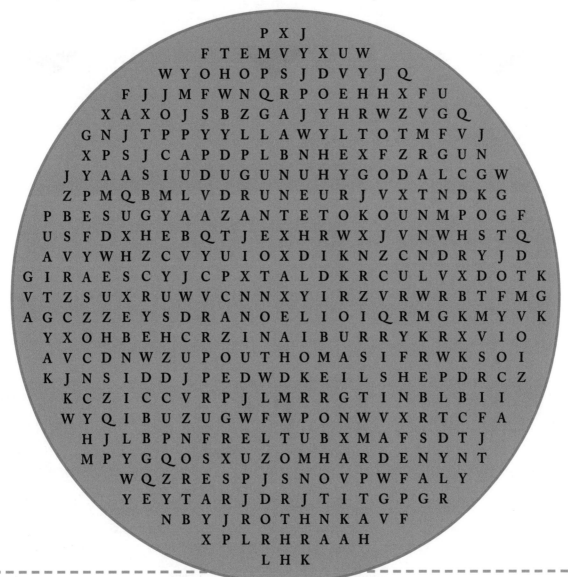

```
            P X J
          F T E M V Y X U W
        W Y O H O P S J D V Y J Q
      F J J M F W N Q R P O E H H X F U
    X A X O J S B Z G A J Y H R W Z V G Q
  G N J T P P Y Y L L A W Y L T O T M F V J
  X P S J C A P D P L B N H E X F Z R G U N
J Y A A S I U D U G U N U H Y G O D A L C G W
Z P M Q B M L V D R U N E U R J V X T N D K G
P B E S U G Y A A Z A N T E T O K O U N M P O G F
U S F D X H E B Q T J E X H R W X J V N W H S T Q
  A V Y W H Z C V Y U I O X D I K N Z C N D R Y J D
G I R A E S C Y J C P X T A L D K R C U L V X D O T K
V T Z S U X R U W C N N X Y I R Z V R W R B T F M G
A G C Z Z E Y S D R A N O E L I O I Q R M G K M Y V K
Y X O H B E H C R Z I N A I B U R R Y K R X V I O
A V C D N W Z U P O U T H O M A S I F R W K S O I
K J N S I D D J P E D W D K E I L S H E P D R C Z
  K C Z I C C V R P J L M R R G T I N B L B I I
W Y Q I B U Z U G W F W P O N W V X R T C F A
  H J L B P N F R E L T U B X M A F S D T J
    M P Y G Q O S X U Z O M H A R D E N Y N T
      W Q Z R E S P J S N O V P W F A L Y
        Y E Y T A R J D R J T I T G P G R
          N B Y J R O T H N K A V F
            X P L R H R A A H
              L H K
```

Antetokounmpo	**DeRozan**	**James**	**Thomas**
Butler	**Durant**	**Jordan**	**Wall**
Curry	**Embiid**	**Leonard**	**Westbrook**
Davis	**Harden**	**Paul**	

Team artist wanted!

A new basketball franchise is coming to your hometown. The team needs a designer pronto! Grab your colored pencils, crayons, or markers and get to work drawing home and away jerseys, shorts, and socks. Let your imagination drive in the paint.

KING ME!

Usually there is nothing wrong with LeBron James's game. "King James" led Cleveland to the 2016 NBA championship, thrilling his hometown fans. But in the bottom picture, things are not kingly. Can you find ten things that have been changed?

LEBRON JAMES
Cleveland Cavaliers

1

2

3

4

5

6

7

8

9

10

THE BEARD

James Harden has become one of the best all-around players in the NBA. He also has the most famous beard in sports. But it's time for his beard to get a new look, and you're the stylist. Use these beardless drawings of Harden to create new looks for him. Will you go with just a mustache? A long beard? Pick any weird shape you want!

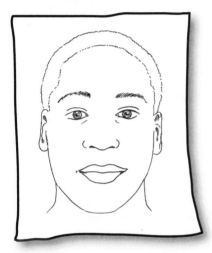 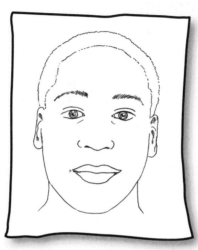 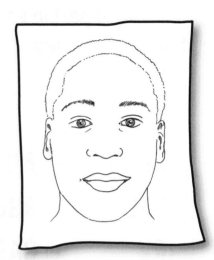

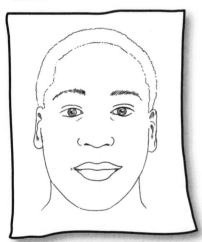 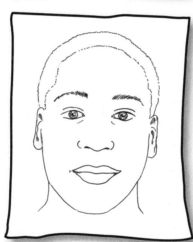 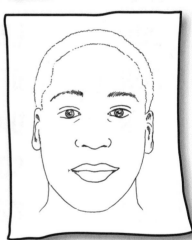

All-Star Fact

This five-time All-Star led the NBA in assists in 2016–2017, averaging more than 11 per game. But Harden was also second in scoring average, with a career-high 29.1 points per game. He has averaged more than 25 points per game in each of the past five seasons.

TEAM BUILDING

Time to build an NBA All-Star team. Take the word parts in Column A and match them with the word parts in Column B to build your winning lineup (last names only). This puzzle is harder than it looks—there is one extra word part in each column that can't be used.

NBA Eastern Conference All-Star team 2017

A

BUT
WAL
IRV
DUR
JOR
HAR
HAY
GEO
KEM
MILL

B

ANT
RGE
SAP
LER
DEN
DAN
SOL
KER
WARD
ING

STAR TEAM

_____

_____

_____

_____

_____

_____

_____

_____

Anthony Davis

FILL THE BUCKET

Go for a two-pointer in this activity. First, fill in the blanks using your knowledge of all things hoop-a-rific. Then unscramble the letters in the circles to figure out the secret basketball term at the bottom.

1. To bounce the ball while running _ _ _ _ _ _ _

2. To bounce the ball off the backboard _ _ _ _ _ _

3. The iron ring players aim for _ _ _ _

4. The lovely sound of the ball going through the net _ _ _ _ _

5. The area under the basket, as in "drive the _ _ _ _"

6. The person who calls the plays and makes the lineup _ _ _ _ _ _

7. Name for a basketball venue _ _ _ _ _

8. An easy shot from close to the basket _ _ _ _ _

○ ○ ○ ○ ○ ○ ○ ○

Pro Tip

"When you dribble, don't let the ball come above your waist. Use your fingertips, not your palm. Keep your eyes up while you dribble."
—NBA All-Star Paul George

Paul George

The NBA All-Stars almost broke the scoreboard in 2017. The West won 192-182 over the East. Defense? Who needs defense?

All-Star Fact

RUSSELL WESTBROOK
Oklahoma City Thunder

TRIPLE-DOUBLE TROUBLE

Oklahoma City All-Star Russell Westbrook stunned the hoops world with his string of triple-doubles in 2016–2017. (A triple-double is recorded when a player hits two-digit figures in three stat categories in an NBA game. In Westbrook's case, it was points, assists, and rebounds.) His feats inspired this puzzle. Can you fill in the missing words in these sports phrases? Hint: each missing word has at least one pair of double letters (like the *t*'s in *letters*).

An NBA mistake: double _____

Nearly making it to the NCAA tournament: on the _____

The fourth guy in a baseball lineup: the cleanup _____

A no-no in hockey and soccer: _____

The last golf club most players use: _____

A max-effort basketball defense: _____ -court _____

The first thing an umpire says: "play _____!"

What Tom Brady plays: _____

Russell Westbrook

All-Star Fact

In 2017, Russell Westbrook set the record for most triple-doubles in a season. He had 42, topping the old mark of 41, which Oscar Robertson set in the 1961–1962 season.

MYSTERY HOOPSTER!

Connect the dots in this puzzle to discover the mysterious basketball superstar. Here's a hint: She was a champion in the NCAA, and now she's a champion in the WNBA. Who is it?

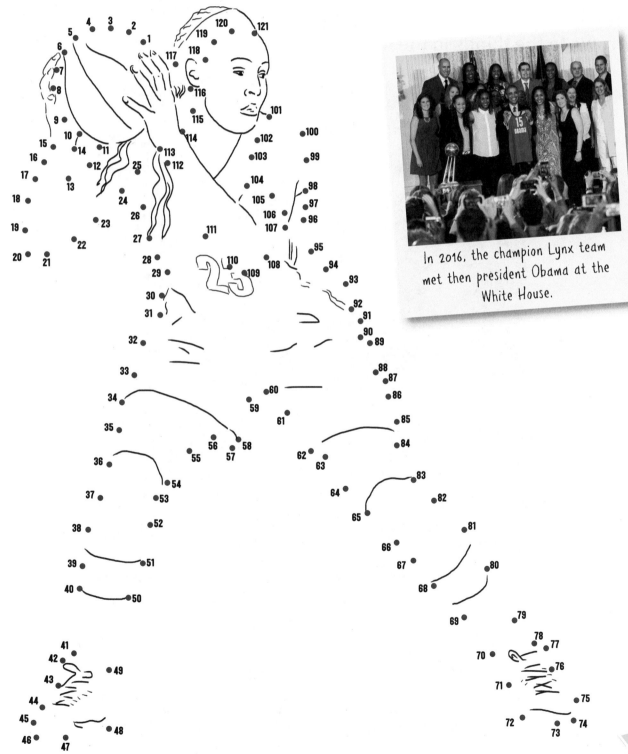

In 2016, the champion Lynx team met then president Obama at the White House.

ROUND MOUND OF REBOUND ASTOUNDS!

Charles Barkley was at it again in the 1991 Eastern Conference Semifinals. He swatted away a basket—and Michael Jordan had feelings about it! Two of these four pictures are exactly the same. Can you find and circle them? While you're at it, draw arrows to the things in the other two pictures that make them different.

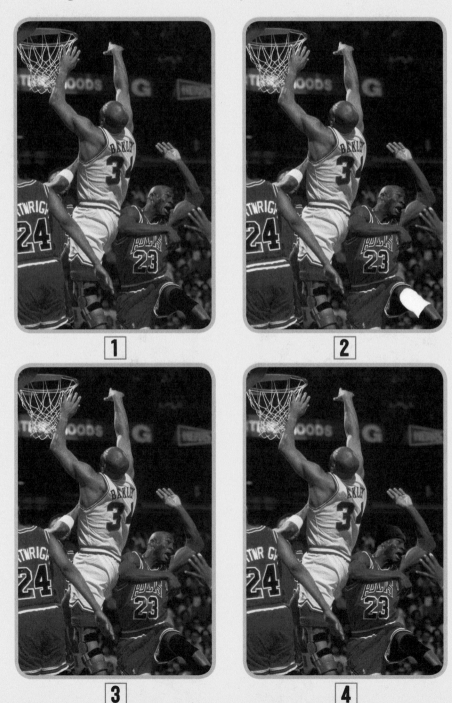

CROSSWORD

Answer the clues and fill in the grid, then take it to the rack!

Across at 6: **T H E**

Across

3. Three-point hero Stephen's last name
5. Bounce the ball . . . and run!
6. LeBron James's nickname
T H E _ _ _ _
9. How each game begins
10. A jam, a flush, a stuff . . . two points!

Down

1. The position that does most of the passing
2. A nickname for the basket that you might find in a kitchen
4. What a player may take after a foul
7. The lane plus the free throw circle
8. A nickname for the backboard
11. A pass that leads to a score

THE CHAMP OF CHAMPS!

In college basketball, the top teams meet in the spring in a pair of men's and women's NCAA tournaments. The teams in each tournament are arranged in a bracket broken up into four regional sections. The winner of each game advances in the bracket. The winner of each region makes it to the Final Four! Out of that group comes the overall champ.

The Connecticut women's team set an all-time record for all top-division NCAA sports by winning 111 straight games from 2014 to 2017.

All-Star Fact

Listed below (but scrambled up!) are some of the colleges that have won the most NCAA championships in men's or women's hoops. Unscramble them and put their names in the blanks. Then unscramble the circled letters to find a secret hoops phrase that describes what champions do!

Men's

LAUC ＿ ＿ ＿ ＿

UKYCTEKN ＿ ＿ ＿(◯)＿ ＿ ＿ ＿

ROTHN ACOANIRL ＿ ＿ ＿ ＿ ＿ ＿ ＿ ＿ ＿ ＿ ＿ ＿ ＿

EUKD ＿ ＿ ＿ ＿

IIAANND ＿(◯)＿ ＿ ＿ ＿ ＿

Women's

TENCCOICNTU ＿ ＿ ＿ ＿ ＿ ＿ ＿ ＿ ＿ ＿ ＿

EEEETSSNN ＿(◯)＿ ＿ ＿ ＿ ＿ ＿ ＿

SUC ＿ ＿ ＿

AANISLOUI CETH ＿ ＿ ＿ ＿(◯)＿ ＿ ＿ ＿ ＿ ＿ ＿

Fill in the blank: CUT DOWN THE ＿ ＿ ＿ ＿!

MARCH MADNESS!

It was sweet victory for the Gamecocks and the Tar Heels in the NCAA basketball tournaments. During the celebrations the winning teams got photobombed! Spot and circle five things in each picture that don't belong.

The Gamecocks were a #1 seed coming into the tournament in 2017. All that pressure paid off when the team brought home the University of South Carolina's first NCAA tournament win.

With its 2017 tournament win—their sixth—the University of North Carolina rose above Duke and Indiana to have a solo hold on the position of third-winningest team in men's college hoops.

Hockey

Check out these puzzles. If you get puck on any of them, it's okay. Make answering them your goal. Okay, enough hockey puns. Strap on your skates and hit the activity ice!

Hall of Fame

GORDIE HOWE

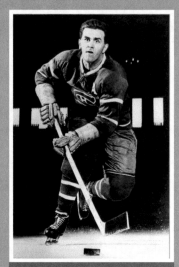

MAURICE RICHARD

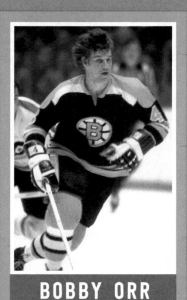

BOBBY ORR

MARIO LEMIEUX

WAYNE GRETZKY

PATRICK ROY

NHL WORD SEARCH

Okay, the first period of the game is over. Time for a break. Get out your hockey stick-shaped pencil and find all the hidden hockey stars in this puck-shaped grid. Look up, down, and diagonally, like a skater on ice. Hurry up before the puck drops for the next period!

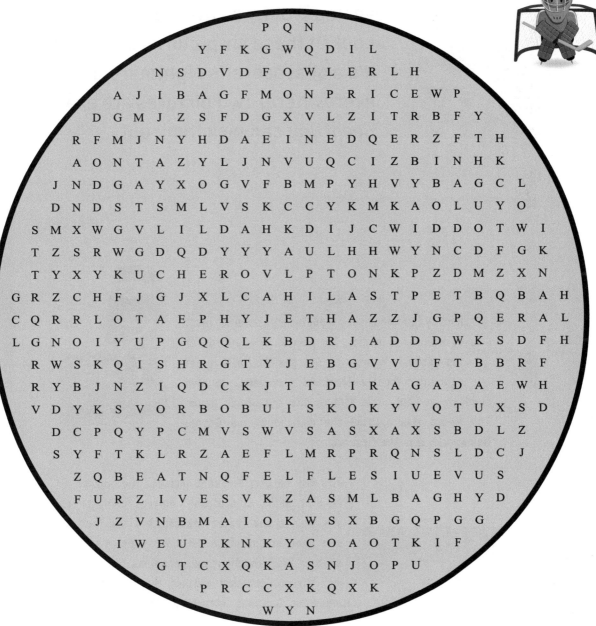

Karlsson	Crosby	Kane	McDavid	Subban
Rask	Simmonds	Laine	Pavelski	Bobrovsky
Price	Tavares	Suter	Doughty	Ovechkin
Kucherov	Holtby	Keith	Fowler	Jágr

GOALIE TWINS

SERGEI BOBROVSKY
Columbus Blue Jackets

Sergei Bobrovsky has been one of the NHL's best goalies in recent seasons. He has been part of two Columbus Blue Jackets playoff teams and has won the Vezina Trophy as the league's top goalie. Look at these six pictures of Bobrovsky. It's a goal scorer's nightmare—Bobrovskys everywhere! Two pictures are exactly alike. See if you can pick them out.

Georges Vezina

All-Star Facts

Hockey is famous for its postseason awards, most of which are named for people. The award for top goalie is named for Georges Vezina, a great netminder for the Montreal Canadiens. He died suddenly in 1926 while still at the top of his game. The award was created the next year and George Hainsworth was the first winner.

The NHL All-Star Weekend includes the popular All-Star Skills Competition. Players compete to see who is the fastest skater, has the hardest slap shot, or can make the most goals in a short span. In 2017, the Montreal Canadiens' Shea Weber won the hardest shot contest. His slap shot was measured traveling more than 102 miles per hour!

Shea Weber

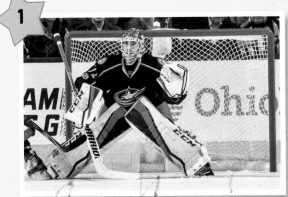

1

2

3

4

5

6

ALL-STAR HOCKEY CHAIN

The best players in the NHL have to be great skaters. In this activity, fill in the path around the rink using the clues. Each circle in the chain gets one letter. The last letter of each word is also the first letter of the next one! Can you make it around the rink in time to score the winning goal?

It's okay to read your answers right side up!

START HERE

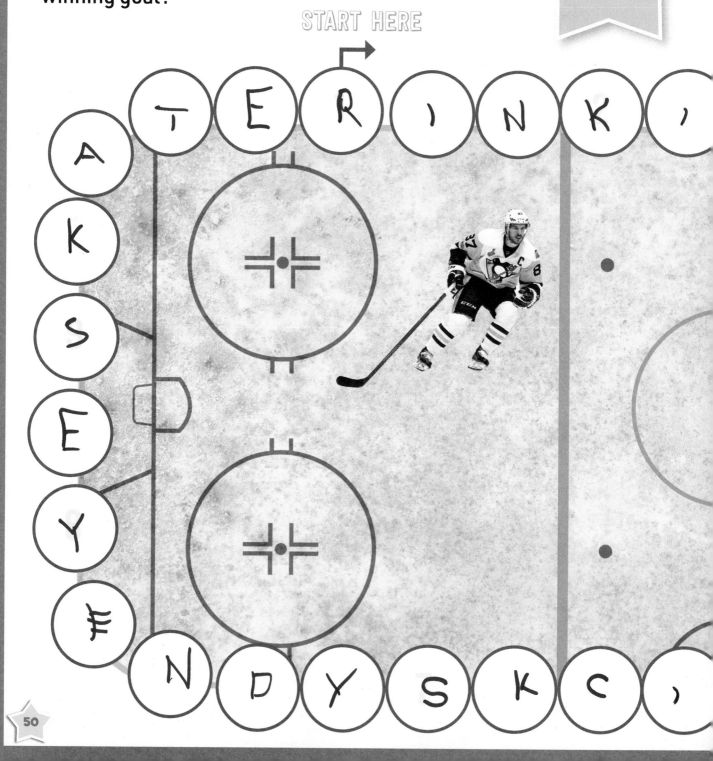

1. Hockey is played on this ice rink
2. The Los Angeles Kings
3. Goalies like to make these saves
4. The most powerful way to shoot SLAP
5. Chicago All-Star Jonathan Towes
6. Players shoot and pass with their Sticks
7. Pittsburgh All-Star Sydney Crosby
8. Yes or no: does a team play with three forwards?
9. To be a great player, you have to be an expert _____

N G S A V E S

L
A
P
space
S
H

T T S E W O T O

O Canada, colorful Canada!

Team Canada needs new designs for their sticks, skates, and sweaters. You are just the artist for the job. Grab your colored pencils, crayons, or markers and get to work. Think beyond white and red!

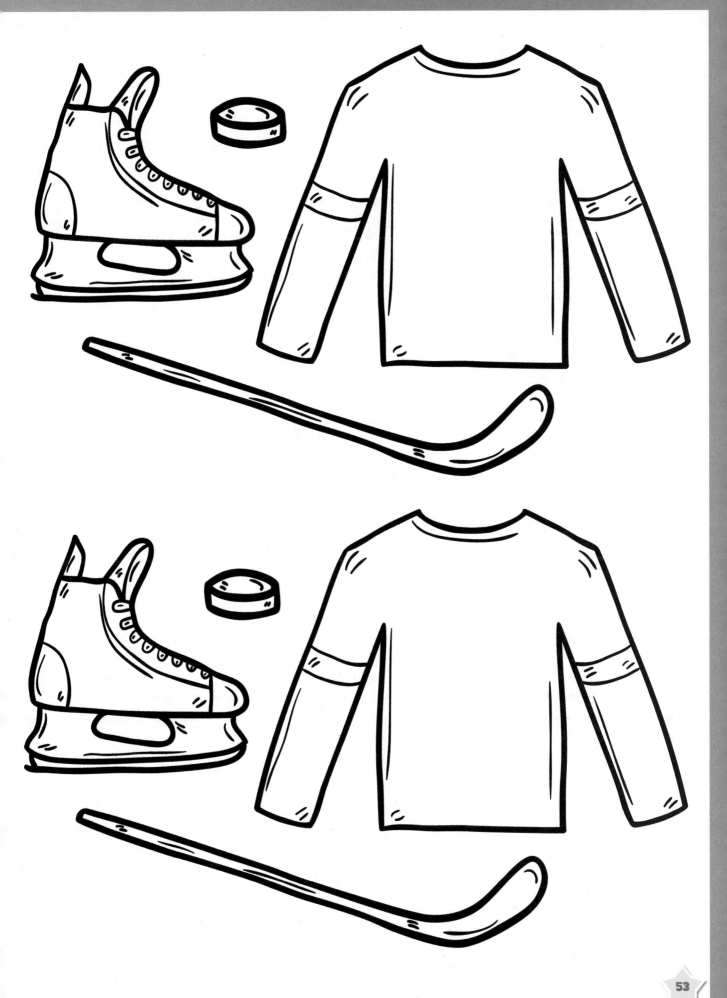

IT'S A MIRACLE!

Get out your pencils and markers, hockey fans! It's time to retell one of the greatest stories in the sport. At the 1980 Winter Olympics, the

It was David vs. Goliath! No one gave the U.S. team a chance!

young U.S. hockey team upset the Soviet Union and went on to win the gold medal. On these pages, use your artistic and writing skills to tell that story . . . in comic-book form!

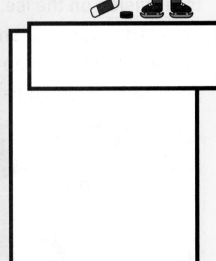

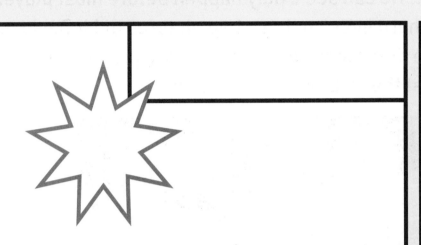

EXTRA! EXTRA! THE U.S. OLYMPIC HOCKEY TEAM BEATS THE SOVIET UNION AND NOW PLAYS FINLAND FOR THE GOLD!

SHARPSHOOTER, SHARP EYES!

Connor McDavid is the hottest young superstar in the NHL. He's superfast, with a superpowerful shot. One of his best skills, though, is his vision on the ice. He can see a play happen before most players are ready! Use your sharp eyes on these two pictures of McDavid in action. There are nine differences between the two pictures. Can you spot them all and hoist the trophy for this puzzle?

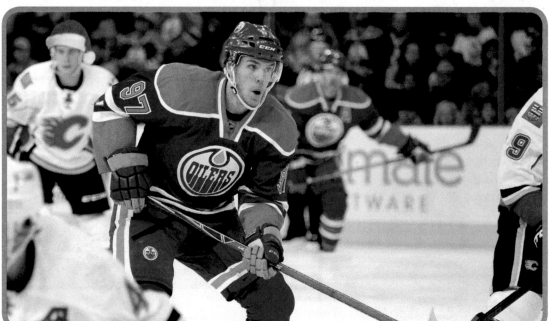

1
2
3
4
5
6
7
8
9

ICY CLEANUP

In between periods at the NHL All-Star Game, it's time to clean the ice. To complete this maze, you have to guide the Zamboni driver all around the ice. Avoid the penguin, polar bear, octopuses, hats, and fish to make it through the finishing gate in time for the next period to start!

All-Star Fact

Why octopuses and hats? In Detroit, Red Wings fans lob octopuses onto the ice late in playoff games. The tradition started long ago, when only eight wins were needed to capture the Stanley Cup. Eight wins, eight legs . . . get it? As for hats, fans throw those onto the ice when one of their players scores his third goal of a game, a feat known as a hat trick.

Sweater weather

There's trouble at the rink. It's time to take an All-Star photo, but the players have mixed up their sweaters. Can you come to the rescue and make sure each player gets into the right team's colors?

Sweaters? That's right: hockey shirts are traditionally called sweaters. That's what the first players wore to keep warm on outdoor rinks. Today, pro players wear polyester to stay cool as they sweat. But longtime fans—especially ones in Canada—still call hockey jerseys sweaters.

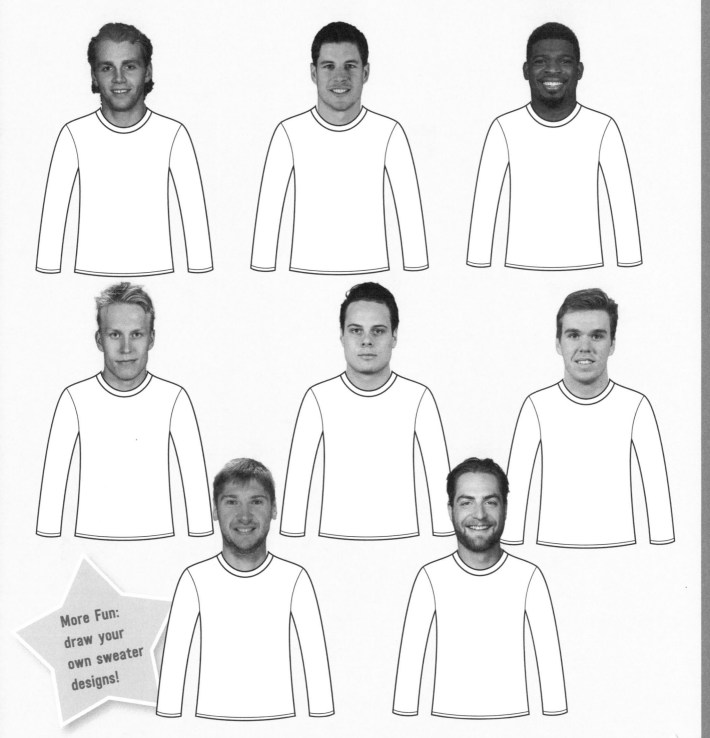

More Fun: draw your own sweater designs!

Soccer

The World Cup is on the line. A billion people are watching—no pressure! For these puzzles, use your head in a different way than players do on the field.

Hall of Fame

PELÉ

DIEGO MARADONA

JOHAN CRUYFF

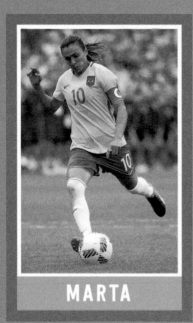

MARTA

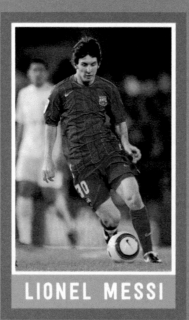

LIONEL MESSI

CRISTIANO RONALDO

SOCCER STARS WORD SEARCH

It's halftime at the soccer match. Your team is up 1–0, so it's still anyone's game. To bring your team some good luck, find all the famous soccer superstars named on this list in the soccer field-shaped grid. Look up, down, diagonally, or backward—just like soccer players run on the field. Once you finish this puzzle, you'll shout, "GOOOOOOOOOOOOOOOOOOALLLLL!"

Vardy	
Ibrahimović	Kroos
Dempsey	Suárez
Pulisic	Piqué
Messi	Neuer
Ronaldo	Iniesta
Morgan	Lloyd
Marta	Honda

```
C  Q  M  E  I  X  H  K  W  M  N  T  U  E  H  I  R  J  L  F
V  I  I  U  I  J  D  O  E  N  T  K  C  I  B  E  F  O  O  L
O  N  S  Q  R  M  V  S  N  A  N  C  S  R  U  N  C  L  Q  C
K  O  E  I  T  V  S  L  L  D  A  T  A  E  U  V  U  L  Q  S
A  D  T  P  L  I  Z  L  H  T  A  H  N  B  O  B  P  A  N  B
W  U  B  F  L  U  I  U  S  G  I  V  W  I  D  L  D  P  L  M
S  Y  I  Y  B  I  P  E  N  M  W  C  Z  J  L  V  V  W  A  K
P  U  Z  S  K  C  I  E  O  S  G  U  S  N  A  A  W  Z  B  Y
M  T  A  I  O  N  S  V  M  O  R  G  A  N  N  R  U  L  V  Y
D  O  E  R  I  O  I  L  L  O  Y  D  W  S  O  D  E  S  N  B
C  C  A  X  E  C  R  Y  E  S  P  M  E  D  R  Y  V  G  Q  C
A  T  R  A  M  Z  K  K  L  O  X  N  U  R  M  E  S  P  V  E
```

All-Star Fact

How would you like it if your favorite team was suddenly demoted to the minor leagues? It happens every year in most soccer leagues around the world. It's called relegation. Teams at or near the bottom of the standings move down a division the next season. The best teams in the lower leagues move up. It creates quite a bit of drama as the final games are played.

QUIZ TIME!

Are you up to speed on soccer basics? Can you go the distance without a substitution? See if you can make the cut by answering these seven questions. *Viva el fútbol!*

1. Soccer is played in _____ halves that are _____ minutes long each.

2. Does the clock in soccer count down to zero or up from zero? _____

3. When the ball gets kicked over the sideline, the other team gets to:
   a. make a corner kick.
   b. throw the ball in.
   c. take a shot on goal.

4. When a goalkeeper stops the ball, it's called a _____.

5. Circle the right answer: Tripping another player is a   fowl   foul   red card.

6. An attacker touches the ball and gets called for a:
   a. foot ball.
   b. penalty touch.
   c. hand ball.

7. Circle the right answer: On average, a pro soccer player runs   3   7   12   miles per match.

WHO SCORED?

It's a race to the goal! Can you follow the twisting paths of these dribbling runs to find out which soccer superstar scored the goal?

Ronaldo

Messi

Dempsey

Tell me a joke!

What did Lionel's mom call his room?

Messi!

GOALKEEPER CONNECTS!

Manuel Neuer connects with the ball in goal more often than not! Start at 1 and connect the dots until a full picture of the German national team captain emerges.

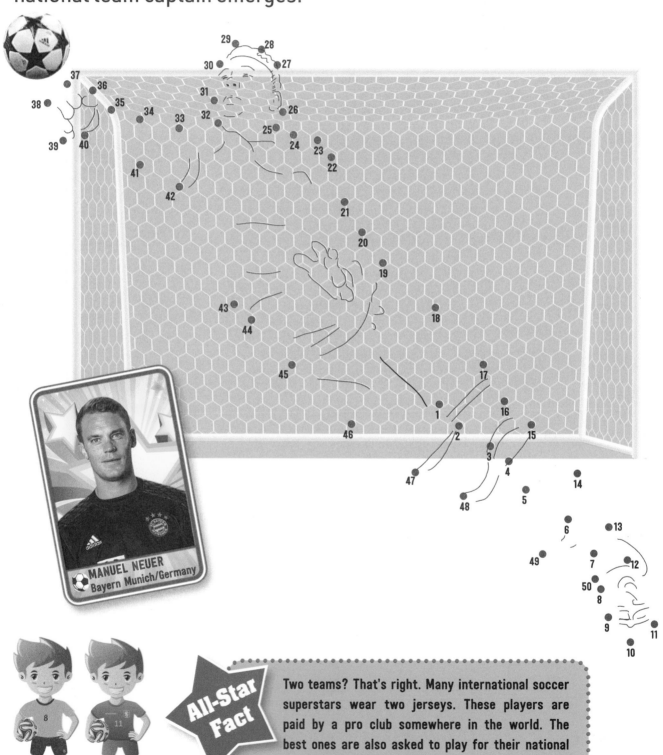

MANUEL NEUER
Bayern Munich/Germany

All-Star Fact

Two teams? That's right. Many international soccer superstars wear two jerseys. These players are paid by a pro club somewhere in the world. The best ones are also asked to play for their national teams against other countries.

SOCCER IS A-MAZE-ING!

Three world soccer superstars are stuck in this maze. Only one will make it out alive! Okay, just kidding—they'll all live—but the two who don't make it have to run extra laps after practice today. Which star makes it to the exit: Yaya Touré of Manchester City and Côte d'Ivoire? Cristiano Ronaldo of Real Madrid and Portugal? Or Michael Bradley of Toronto FC and the U.S. national team? Gentlemen, start your dribbles!

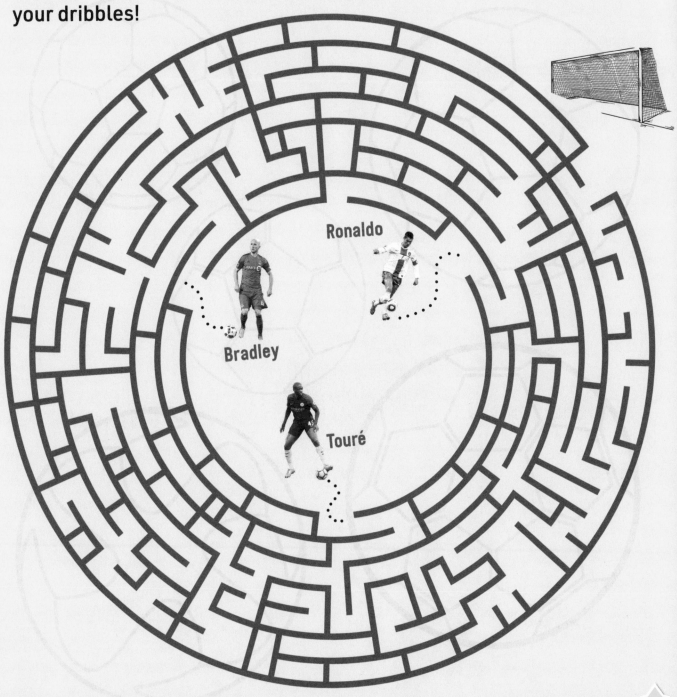

Rainbow balls

Remember when soccer balls were only black and white? Nah, me neither. Grab your colored pencils, crayons, or markers and get to work making sick multicolored designs on these boring soccer balls.

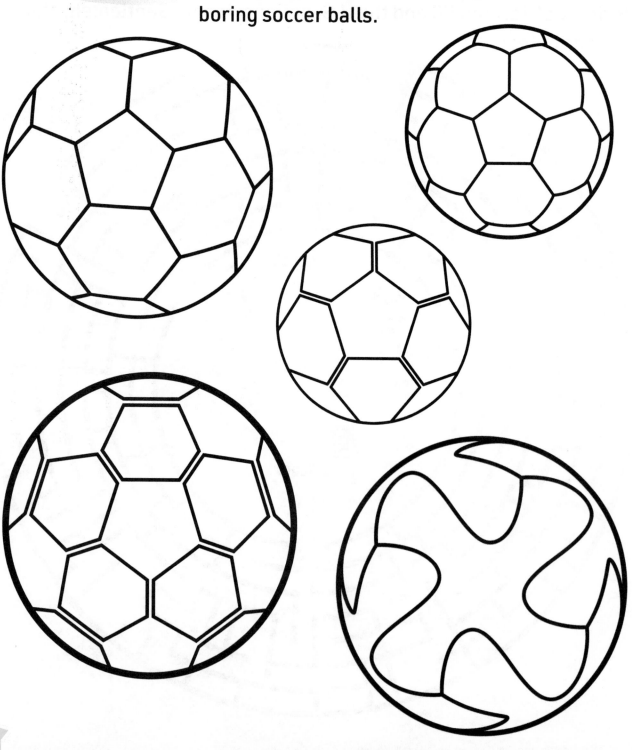

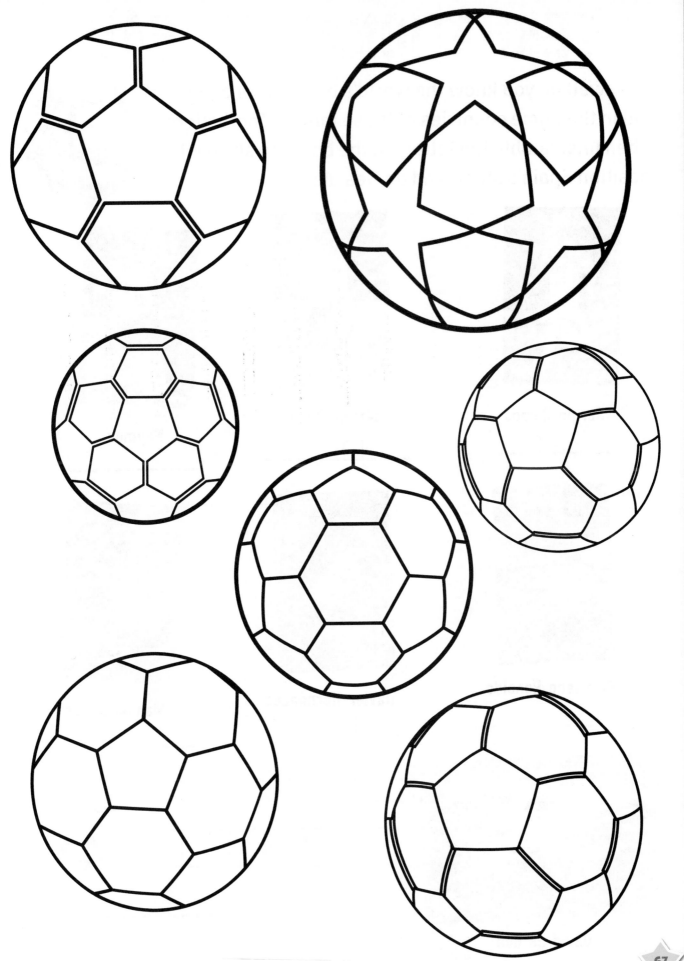

INTERNATIONAL APPEAL

How well do you know the world's best soccer all-stars?
Fill in the home countries of these famous footballers.
Then unscramble the letters in the boxes to show what
position Spain's star David de Gea plays!

Sergio Ramos

_ _ _ ☐ _

Wayne Rooney

_ _ ☐ _ _ _ _

Neymar

_ _ _ _ _ ☐

Cristiano Ronaldo

_ ☐ _ _ _ _ _ _

Javier Hernández

_ ☐ _ _ _ _

Manuel Neuer

_ _ _ _ ☐ _

David de Gea

☐ ☐ ☐ ☐ ☐ ☐

SOCCER STUFF!

Use the clues to fill in the grid and dribble your way to victory!

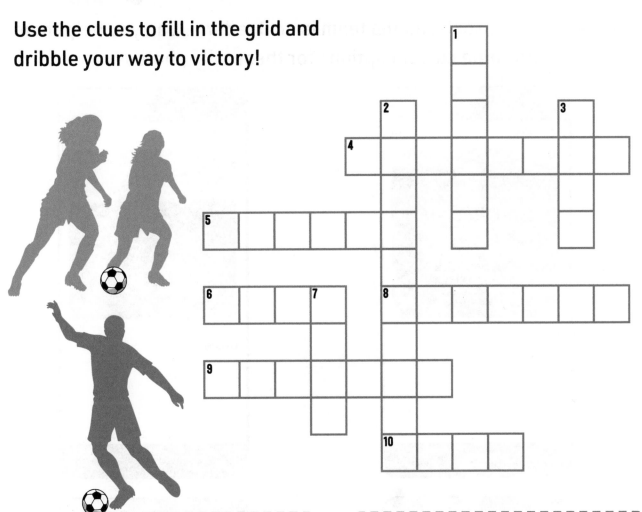

Across

4. Soccer's biggest international championship
5. The number of players on a full-size team
6. A good way to get the ball to a teammate
8. The 23rd person on the field
9. The way to put the ball back in play from the sidelines
10. What you usually do to a soccer ball

Down

1. The only player who can use his or her hands
2. What happens when the defense kicks the ball over its own end line
3. What a goalkeeper does to get the ball way down the field
7. The name for the place from which penalty kicks are taken

TOM GOOFS AROUND

Thomas Müller's social media team is on deadline. Can you help them out by writing some clever captions for these silly photos?

CORNER KICK LOOK-AND-FIND

See if you can get ahead of this friendly match between Team U.S.A. and the Russian national team by finding and circling all the things in the picture that don't belong. Can you find all ten?

1	2	3	4	5	6	7	8	9	10

LAUNDRY DAY MIX-UP!

It's laundry day at the World Cup, and all the jerseys are mixed up. Can you deliver the correct national team jersey to the player who wears it? Luckily, this batch of players is from all different countries.

All-Star Fact

The FIFA World Cup has been played 20 times. Only 8 nations have won the title, though. Of those, 3 have been especially dominant: Brazil (5), Germany (4), and Italy (4) have taken 13 of the 20 titles.

Golf

Mark Twain wrote: "Golf is a good walk spoiled." Mr. Twain, we beg to differ. Sure, golf is tough to master, but sharpen your golf pencil and you'll be sure to knock these puzzles right in the hole.

Hall of Fame

BEN HOGAN

ARNOLD PALMER

JACK NICKLAUS

NANCY LOPEZ

ANNIKA SORENSTAM

TIGER WOODS

SERGIO EARNS THE GREEN

It may have taken 18 years, but pro golfer Sergio García finally won a major in 2017. Celebrate with García as he wins the Masters in a playoff. While García is off getting fitted for his green jacket, spot all the differences in these two photos of his big moment.

1
2
3
4
5
6
7
8
9
10

DOTS ON THE BALL

A golf ball can have as many as 500 "dimples" on it. Most models have between 300 and 400. The dimples are tiny, shallow divots. They help air flow more smoothly over the ball and help it go straight. This ball has a special pattern of dots. See if you can connect them in order to get a picture of one of the top players on the LPGA Tour.

LEXI THOMPSON
LPGA golfer

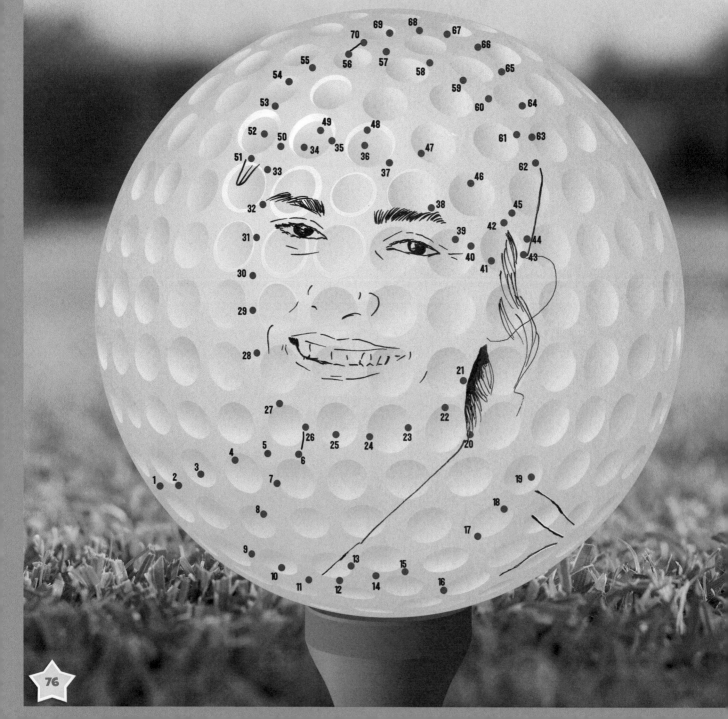

GOLF ACROSTIC

Every male golfer dreams of winning one of the four major championships. To discover the names of those big four, fill in the answers to these clues. Then put the letters in the boxes matching the numbers under them. The result will be the names of the four majors.

1. A place to fish ___ ___ ___ ___ ___ ___
13   4   9   23   27   1

2. Something cowboys wear to ride ___ ___ ___ ___ ___
28   29   2   22   7

3. What a beautiful ___ ___ ___ ___ ___ **this is**
36   10   26   37   11

4. A place to put laundry ___ ___ ___ ___ ___ ___
29   30   31   25   17   6

5. Something added on to raise the prize ___ ___ ___ ___ ___
8   15   35   19   20

6. The opposite of *closes* ___ ___ ___ ___ ___
21   32   5   18   3

7. A rabbit moving; rhymes with *boppin'* ___ ___ ___ ___ ___ ___
14   34   39   16   12   24

1	2	3	4	5	6	7

8	9	10	11	12	13	14	15	16	17	18

19	20	21	22	23	24

25	26	27	28	29	30	31	32	i	34	35	36	37	i	39

PAR FOR THE COURSE

There is a new golf course in Pebble Beach, California, but the architect needs your help. She wants you to design the course. Yup! Don't forget to include the tee box, the fairway, sand traps, water holes, bunkers, and the putting green. Fore!

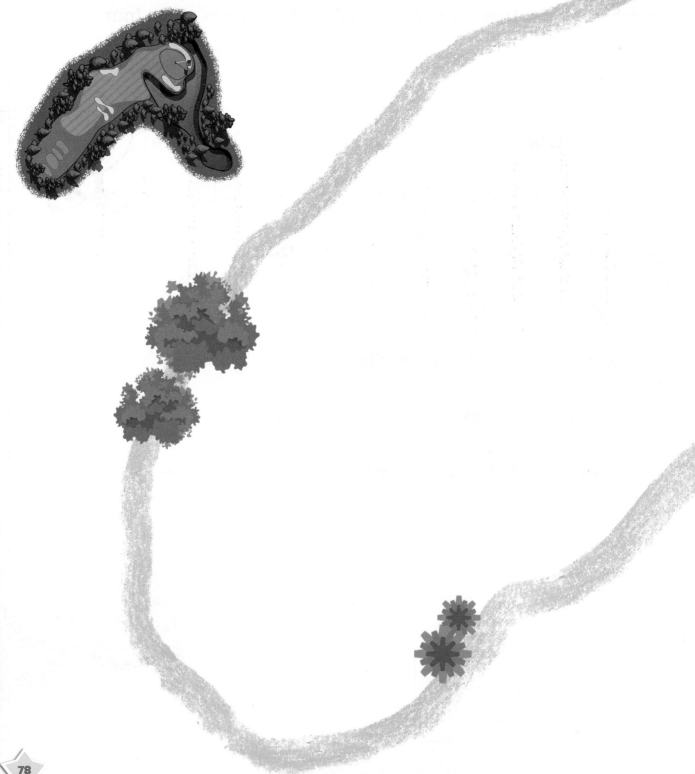

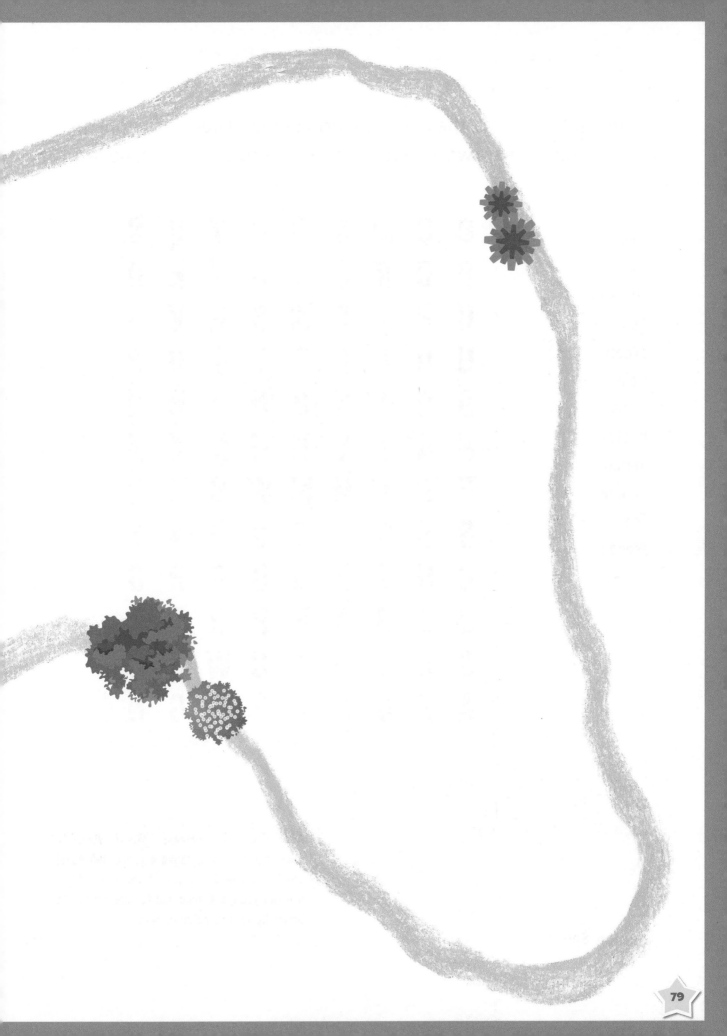

READY FOR YOUR TEE TIME!

Find the golf terms on the list in the grid below. They each appear once and might be forward, backward, or diagonal. Search out all 12!

Ball
Cart
Fairway
Flag
Green
Hole
Irons
Putter
Rough
Spikes
Tee
Woods

```
O G M S G J Y Q S
P D R S A A Y E Q
U R I E W S E V A
U D L R E T T U P
B O I K O N J U U
H A I Y N N M Z Z
F P L M M W S C D
S B S L D S D A Y
B N T H G U O R J
J G B A E P O T K
D L L O I D W F J
A F U P L F G G N
```

Jordan Spieth

All-Star Fact

According to *Guinness World Records*, Christian Carpenter (aged 4 years, 195 days) and Soona Lee-Tolley (aged 5 years, 103 days) are the youngest male and female golfers to officially record holes in one.

MATCH PLAY

Now that you know all your golf terms, let's get ready for your morning tee time. Match the words from the list below to this jumble of equipment and golf course locations by drawing lines between them. There's one image not on the list. What is it?
Write your answer here: _____

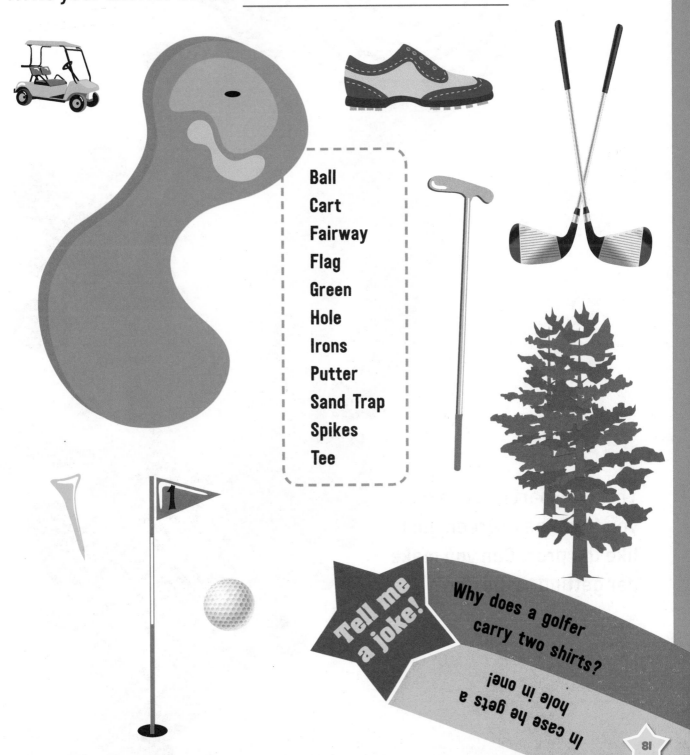

Ball
Cart
Fairway
Flag
Green
Hole
Irons
Putter
Sand Trap
Spikes
Tee

Tell me a joke!

Why does a golfer carry two shirts?

In case he gets a hole in one!

FROM TEE TO GREEN— THE LONG WAY!

This two-part maze takes you from tee to green, just like the pros. Can you make par getting to the flag?

start

GOLFER'S DELIGHT

Pick up your sticks and see if you can answer all these clues and fill in the grid. Fore!

Across

2. Larger clubs usually used to drive the ball
4. The large area of grass between tee and green
6. A club that a player uses on the green
9. A score of one under par on a hole
10. A nickname for a hole in one

Down

1. A score of one over par on a hole
3. The little divots on the surface of the ball
5. A person who carries golf clubs and assists a player
7. A small thing that holds a golf ball for a driver
8. What most people use to get around a golf course
9. Another name for a sand trap

Tennis

The Arena Court is jammed with fans, but they have gone silent. Your opponent, Ivan Puzzleitch, tosses up the ball. His serve sizzles across the net. You whip your pencil forward—you win!

Hall of Fame

ROD LAVER

MARTINA NAVRATILOVA

CHRIS EVERT

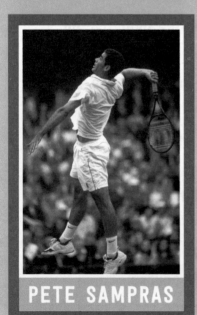

PETE SAMPRAS

ROGER FEDERER

SERENA WILLIAMS

SISTERS ARE DOIN' IT FOR THEMSELVES!

This duo has been dominating women's tennis for nearly 20 years. Playing together, they've won 174 of their 204 doubles matches. On their own, they've won a combined total of 30 Grand Slam titles. Who are these tennis powerhouses? Connect the dots to find out!

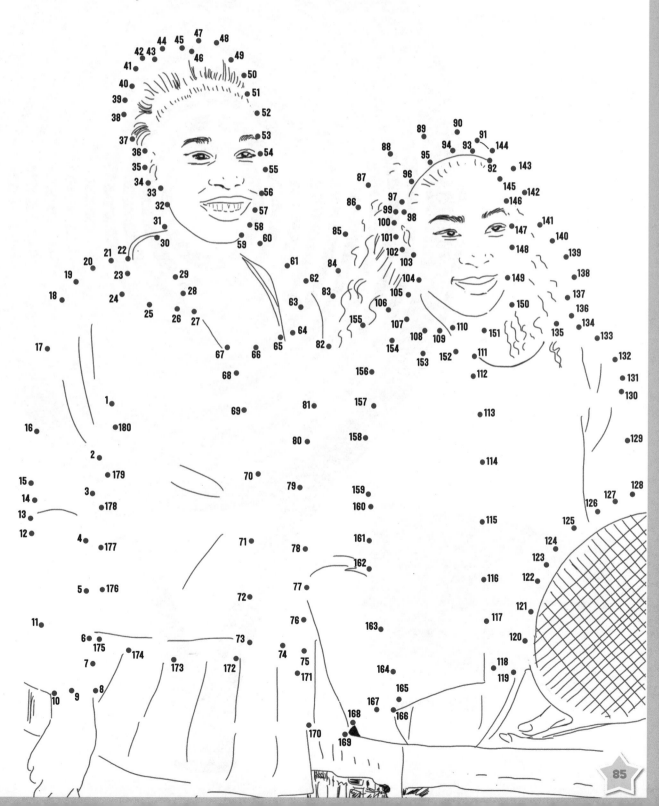

WHAT A RACKET!

Someone restrung this racket and did a terrible job! Can you solve the maze to untangle this mess? Start in the center and work your way out.

Rafael Nadal

WIMBLEDON LOOK-AND-FIND

Roger Federer just won his eighth Wimbledon trophy! But something has gone wrong at the award ceremony after the final match. See if you can find and circle all ten things that don't belong on Centre Court.

1

2

3

4

5

6

7

8

9

10

Althea Gibson recorded a lot of firsts. She was the first black woman to win at Wimbledon, the first black woman to be honored with a ticker-tape parade in New York City, and—after she retired from tennis—the first black woman to play on the Ladies Professional Golf Association Tour.

Game, set, match!

Your summer camp is holding a tennis tournament in July. You are in charge of creating a poster to advertise the event. Singles, doubles, and mixed doubles are welcome. Don't forget to serve up some creativity!

Some ideas for the poster:

GAME, SET, MIX, AND MATCH!

Time to test your tennis superstar knowledge. Some of the world's best players are all on this tennis court. It's not just the players who are mixed up, though. So are their names! Unscramble the names in the spaces provided, using the player images for hints. Then take the circled letters and use them to make the name of tennis's greatest feat!

Players

R S E E (A) N   (M) A L I W L S I   _____

A A F R L E   (N) D A A L   _____

D (A) Y N   (R) A M R U Y   _____

I N A (G) E E U L Q   E E K R R B   _____

E U V N S   (S) W I M I (L) L A   _____

E R G R O   R R E E F (D) E   _____

Secret words: _____

(Hint: there are four tournaments in this.)

YOU'LL LOVE THIS CROSSWORD

Time for some tennis! Answer the clues and fill in the grid to win the match!

Across

3. Tennis played with a partner
4. England's famous home of tennis
5. The back of each side of the court
6. The group name for the four major pro tournaments
9. What you hit the ball with

Down

1. A score of zero in a game
2. A high, arcing shot
3. Two service errors in a row
7. One of the great Williams sisters
8. A serve that stays in but that your opponent doesn't even touch!

Olympics

The Olympic motto is "faster, higher, stronger." In this chapter, you can be "smarter, funnier, brainier." We made that last one up, but you won't make up any answers to these puzzles and activities!

Hall of Fame

PAAVO NURMI

JESSE OWENS

MARK SPITZ

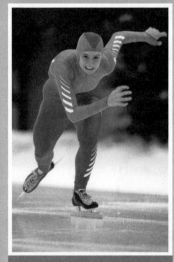

BONNIE BLAIR

MICHAEL PHELPS

USAIN BOLT

GO FOR THE GOLD!

Okay, here's a real Olympic challenge. Make some copies of this page and have an Olympics puzzle-solving contest. Challenge your friends to see who can find all 20 of these Olympic sports the fastest. Award gold, silver, and bronze medals to the top three finishers! Of course, you can also play the national anthem on your phone at the awards ceremony!

Word List:

- Archery
- Basketball
- Biathlon
- Boxing
- Curling
- Cycling
- Decathlon
- Diving
- Fencing
- Golf
- Gymnastics
- Hockey
- Judo
- Luge
- Rowing
- Sailing
- Soccer
- Swimming
- Tennis
- Volleyball

```
O O E D O N G A P O P U Y L X V R C S M W C
L N D K J J D N G P R Q L W O S U O Q U G A
P N L T V U W V I Q Q A E L T R C O Y B S E
Z O X U P K J O H M B X L R L C S S Z Q D G
L Y I V U D L P G T M E D I E I N I U S J G
D D A S T W M Q E N Y I N R E Z G N Z R U L
H U F I L M Q K O B I G W G S X N N Y S U S
X D W K O C S G A G N V V S X J I E S G R H
O N P V Q A S L N X N B I M R X X T E E D X
R Q U E B A L N G N L I Q D M P O E S V A W
G T Z A I S O B J F U I C A I Q B S I B S X
R I C L E Q M S N K R B P N G I Z V R Y V O
Y Z I K E K V N Z W F O F N E R O Z Y T U H
G N K K A N G B M C N C W B O F B O P V G R
G O U D Y D G N W H O D H I B L D W B E F P
D B Q U T W H N S C L O O E N U H S L V T Y
S C I T S A N M Y G H D C Z J G C T W L P P
M O W C H L L Y G E T Q K N K L X T A Z J N
A T K Q L P S G B J A Q E Y R Y R E H C R A
X N J N I P H P U J I U Y Z D A T L C K E K
K L S N B U C L R H B W N I S N Z V U Q S D
C Y C L I N G F L O G T X B O X Q Q T X E T
```

All-Star Fact

The modern Olympics began in 1896. They were held in Athens, Greece, which was the site of the ancient Olympics more than 3,000 years ago! And no, basketball was not on the ancient Olympic list of sports!

PERFECT!

Simone Biles is probably the best gymnast of all time. She's a three-time World Champion and won four gold medals at the 2016 Summer Olympics. One reason that she is so good is that she can do things over and over again perfectly. Look at these six pictures of Biles and find the two that are exactly alike!

SIMONE BILES
Team U.S.A.

Aly Raisman, Madison Kocian,
Laurie Hernandez, Gabby Douglas,
and Simone Biles

Did you know?
The 2016 U.S. gymnastics team, known as the Final Five, broke the Olympic team record by winning nine medals in Rio. The previous record of eight medals was set in 1984 and matched in 2008.

Tell me a joke!

Gymnast: Can you teach me to do a split leap?

Coach: How flexible are you?

Gymnast: I can't make Tuesdays.

1

2

3

4

5

6

CONNECTION ON THE ICE

It was gold at Sochi in 2014 for the U.S. ice dancing champs Meryl Davis and Charlie White. Connect the dots to create a portrait-perfect image of their athletic artistry.

MERYL DAVIS / CHARLIE WHITE
Team U.S.A.

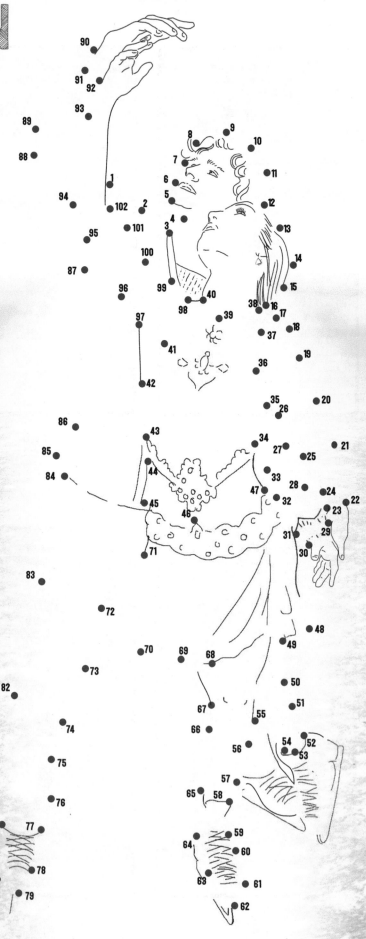

ESCAPE FROM THE POOL!

At the 2016 Summer Olympics, the women's 100-meter freestyle had a rare result: a tie! Team U.S.A.'s Simone Manuel and Canada's Penny Oleksiak both finished in exactly 52.70 seconds. That was a new Olympic record! They gave each other a wet high five and a hug before climbing out of the pool. But they need your help to do that. Manuel and Oleksiak have to find their way out of this maze. Trace the path to get them out so they can claim their gold medals (yes, they each got one!).

All-Star Facts

Each swimmer touches a special electronic pad at the end of a race. It stops the clock for that swimmer, so race officials know who had the fastest times.

In this race, Simone was the first African American woman to earn a medal in Olympic swimming. She later added another gold in the 4x100 medley relay and a pair of silvers, to leave Rio with four medals overall!

Olympic Logo Contest

Your hometown has won the bid to host the 2040 Summer Olympic Games! The Olympic Committee is counting on you to design the logo. This is a big responsibility, but you are up to the challenge. Don't forget to add in your town's name, color in the rings, and add a mascot character, if you like.

Some ideas for the logo:

Baron Pierre de Coubertin

A WET MESS

How well do you follow directions? Using the word grid below, follow the directions carefully. When you're finished, the remaining letters should spell out the names of some U.S. Olympic swimming stars.

MIGOLDCHAQELABCPHEZLPSABCKAQTISWIMEABCLZ

EDECKYSISWIMMONEZMAQNSWIMUELABCZANTHQONZ

YERSWIMVINMISABCSYGOLDFZRAQNGOLDKLINSWIM

1. Cross out the Zs.
2. Cross out all combinations of A-B-C.
3. Cross out any Qs.
4. Look for the words "swim" and "gold" and cross them out.

Answers

1. _____

2. _____

3. _____

4. _____

5. _____

All-Star Fact

Make your travel plans now! Here are the locations of upcoming Olympic Games, plus room for you to fill in one name. Look it up!

2018 Winter Games: PyeongChang, South Korea

2020 Summer Games: Tokyo, Japan

2022 Winter Games: Beijing, China

2024 Summer Games: _____

GOLD-MEDAL CROSSWORD

All hail the Olympics! Climb the podium by answering these clues and filling in the grid.

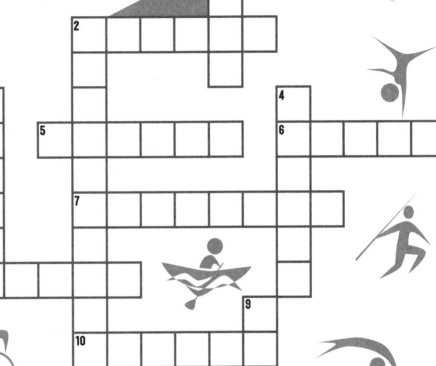

Across

2. The country where the ancient Olympics were held
5. This is played during the medal ceremony
6. The Olympic logo has five of these
7. Michael Phelps's Olympic sport
8. The country home to the 2016 Olympics
10. The medal for second place

Down

1. The flaming symbol of the Games
2. Simone Biles's Olympic sport
3. It's not Summer, it's _____
4. The medal for third place
9. Usain Bolt's Olympic sport

SNOWY MAZE

Olympic gold medalist Mikaela Shiffrin is an expert at the slalom. But this maze might challenge even her amazing skills. Can you help her find the way from the top of the mountain to the ski lodge? Watch out for the yeti!

MIKAELA SHIFFRIN
Team U.S.A.

All-Star Fact

World Cup skiers take part in four types of races: downhill, slalom, giant slalom, and super G. There is also a fifth competition that combines downhill and slalom. Racers get points based on how they finish. At the end of the season, a champion is crowned in each of the five competitions. The skier with the most points from all races is the World Cup champion.

OLYMPIC REPORT

The Olympics is packed with events, and it's hard for anyone to follow them all. But you're an ace reporter and you can zip from event to event. Let your readers know what happened by filling in the blanks.

_____ reporting _____ from _____,
<u>name</u>   <u>adverb</u>   <u>city</u>

site of the _____ Olympics.
<u>adjective</u>

The first event today was track and _____. The winner was from _____,
<u>noun</u>   <u>country</u>

after she _____ _____ feet. It was a new _____
<u>past tense verb</u>   <u>number</u>   <u>noun</u>

record. Next up, swimming! The _____ medalist in the _____-meter
<u>color</u>   <u>big number</u>

_____ stroke won by a _____. Then, during a volleyball _____, a
<u>animal</u>   <u>body part</u>   <u>noun</u>

player _____ the _____ so hard that it _____!
<u>past tense verb</u>   <u>noun</u>   <u>past tense verb</u>

Finally, I _____ to the _____ Arena for
<u>past tense verb</u>   <u>name of your gym teacher</u>

gymnastics. The _____ gymnast needed to be _____ to win.
<u>nationality</u>   <u>adjective</u>

She _____, _____, _____! The _____ judges put up the
<u>three past tense verbs</u>   <u>nationality</u>

_____. She got a _____! To celebrate, she _____!
<u>noun</u>   <u>number</u>   <u>past tense verb</u>

# All-Stars

The athletes below don't necessarily come from sports that have "all-star" designations, but they all have amazing stories and are definitely all-time greats in their sport—or sports!—of choice.

Sports Greats

MUHAMMAD ALI

SHAUN WHITE

TONY HAWK

HAILE GEBRSELASSIE

RONDA ROUSEY

BETHANY HAMILTON

GIVE IT YOUR ALL (STAR)!

All-Star is made of two parts: the *all* and the *star*! For this puzzle, we'll spot you the *all*, and you fill in the rest to complete the words. Use the clues below from around the world of sports to fill in the blanks.

Tell me a joke!

Why did Bill Belichick go to the bank?

To get his quarterback.

1. John _ A L L — Wizards assist-happy guard

2. _ A L L _ _ _ _ — Where Aaron Judge does his work

3. _ _ A L L _ _ left field — Where Corey Dickerson might bloop a double

4. _ A L L _ — A cap worn in an unconventional manner to will a team to victory

5. _ A L L _ _ _ — A kind of duck—a real one, not an Anaheim one like Cam Fowler!

6. _ _ _ _ _ _ _ A L L — A pitch nicknamed "Uncle Charlie" that Lance McCullers loves to throw

7. _ A L L — Eric Lindros is a recent inductee into the Hockey _____ of Fame

New City, New Teams

It was amazing! A huge new island suddenly appeared off the coast of Florida. People moved to New Wave City right away. Of course, they wanted sports teams. Here's your chance to help those new teams. For each league, make up a team name and draw a logo. What themes will you use? What colors? It's up to you!

New Wave City

 NFL

Team name _____

 NBA

Team name _____

WNBA

Team name _____

MLB

Team name _____
_____

MLS

Team name _____
_____

All-Star Fact

Trivia time: Which two of the following cities do NOT have at least one team in each of the five leagues listed above? **Minneapolis, Atlanta, Portland, Dallas, Denver**

Meme it!

Write captions for these hilarious sports photos.
To make it a contest, ask your friends to write captions, and
then judge which ones make you LOL the hardest.

José Lobatón,
Washington Nationals

Germany's Thomas Müller (left)
and France's Patrice Evra

Tell me a joke!

Why are babies good at basketball?

They're always dribbling!

LeBron James,
Cleveland Cavaliers

Andy Murray,
Scottish tennis player

Design the gear, dude!

Your local skateboard shop is having a contest, and your canvas is your brand-new skateboard. Use the blank skateboards below to design an original look. Get creative! The winner will get to see his or her design printed on a new line of skateboards available at the shop next spring.

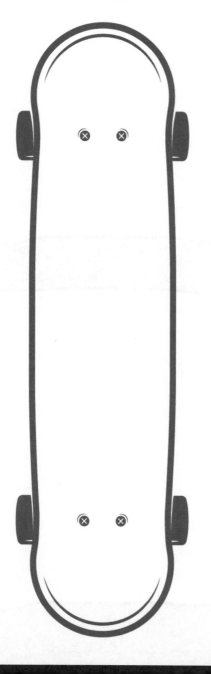
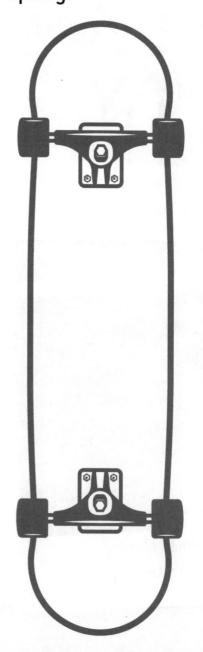

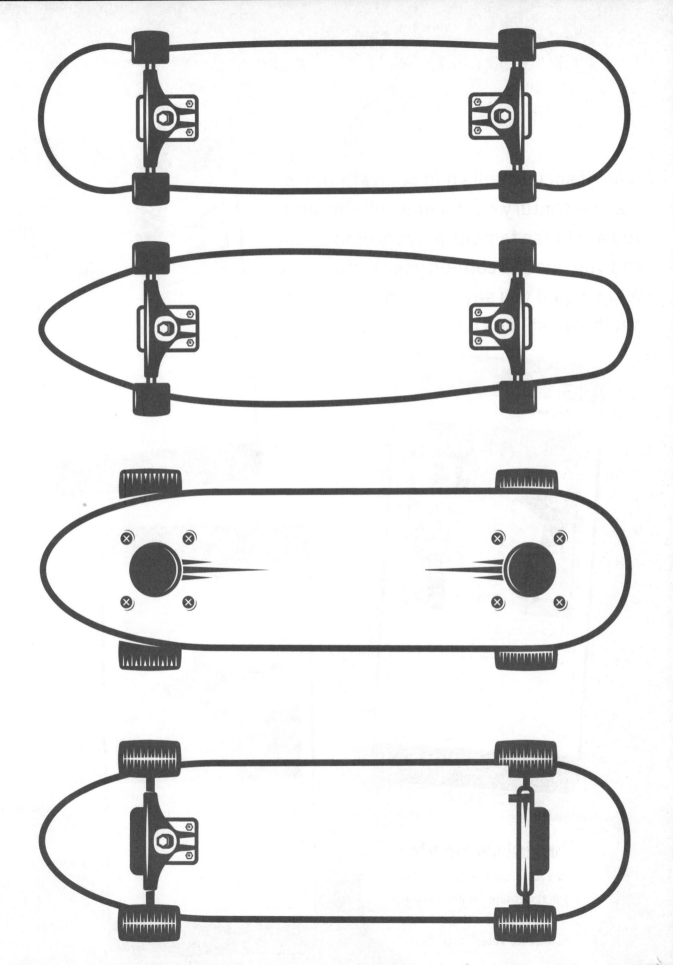

SOCIAL MEDIA TIME MACHINE

What if social media had been around in the last century? Let's find out. Pretend you are these famous players of the past and you need to caption your pictures. What would you say about these photos to get the most likes from your followers?

Quotable quote!
"You better cut the pizza in four pieces because I'm not hungry enough to eat six."
—Lawrence Peter "Yogi" Berra

MuhammadAli •••

👍 💬 ↩

Liked by

WiltChamberlain •••

👍 ❤ 💬 ↩

Liked by

JackNicklaus •••

👍 💬 ↩

Liked by

ArnoldPalmer •••

👍 ❤ 💬 ↩

Liked by

SPOT THE DIFFERENCE AT THE KENTUCKY DERBY

Riding atop Always Dreaming, jockey John Velazquez has to have sharp vision. Take off your blinders and study these two images closely.

Tell me a joke!

Did you hear about the kid who was hospitalized for swallowing six toy horses?

The doctor said his condition is stable.

There are eight differences between these two pictures of the winner's circle following the 143rd running of the Kentucky Derby. Can you spot all eight and hoist the trophy for this puzzle? Maybe your friends will shower you with champagne and roses afterward!

NASCAR COIN FLIP

For this race, all you need is a penny. (Well, any coin will do, but pennies are easy to find!) You and a friend each pick one of the NASCAR racers on this track: Kurt Busch or Kyle Busch. The youngest player goes first. Take turns flipping the penny. Follow the chart to find out how many spaces you get to move ahead (or not!). The first one to reach the finish line is the winner!

Kyle Busch   Kurt Busch

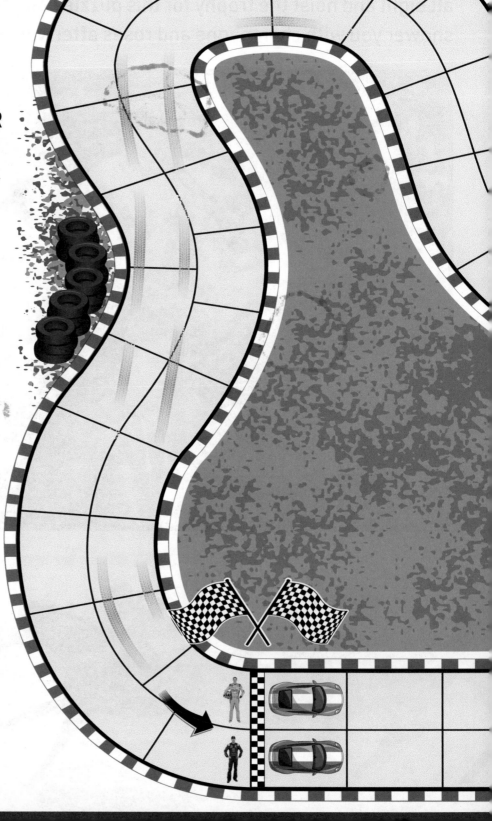

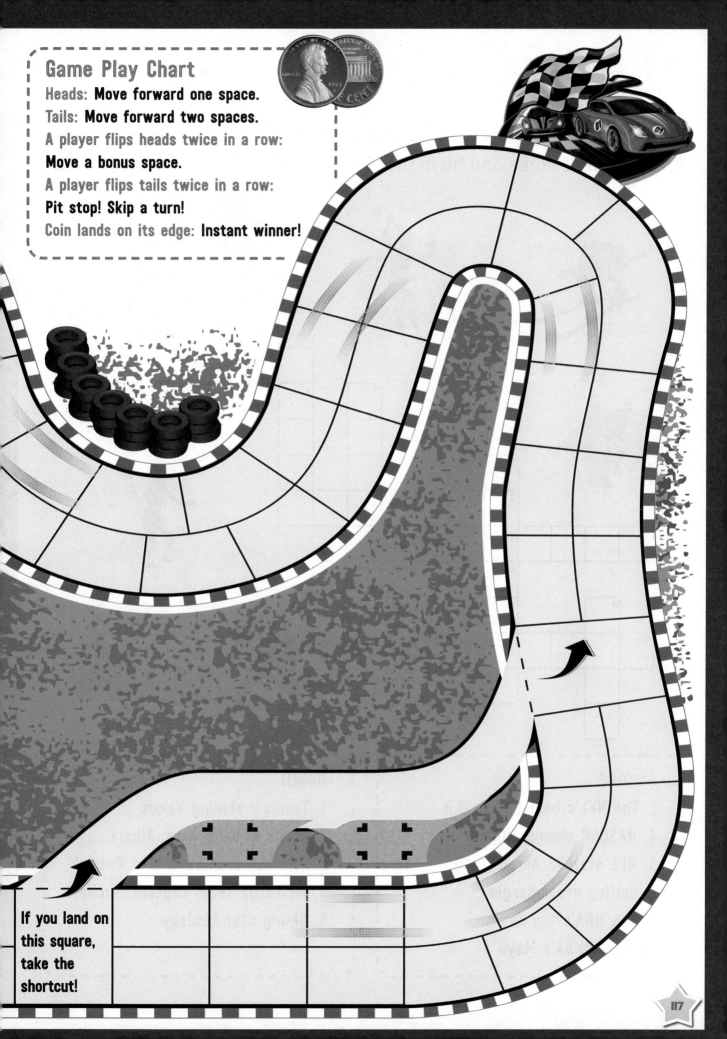

Game Play Chart

Heads: Move forward one space.

Tails: Move forward two spaces.

A player flips heads twice in a row: **Move a bonus space.**

A player flips tails twice in a row: **Pit stop! Skip a turn!**

Coin lands on its edge: **Instant winner!**

If you land on this square, take the shortcut!

ALL-STAR CROSSWORD

How well do you know your all-stars?
Answer these clues and fill in the last names.

Across
1. The NFL's best-known J.J.
4. NASCAR champ Jimmie
6. NFL star QB Aaron
7. Golfing great Sergio
8. The NBA's top Kevin
10. The WNBA's Maya

Down
1. Tennis's shining Venus
2. MLB's 600-HR man, Albert
3. The NHL's Chicago star Patrick
5. MLS's US team captain, Michael
9. Skiing star Lindsey

ANSWERS

PAGE 5
1. 4 + 2 − 2 = 4
2. 30 − (4 x 1) = 26
3. 4 x 4 = 16
4. 3 x 6 − 3 = 15
5. 3 x (3 + 9) = 36

PAGE 6

```
            R F E
        F I O G R I F E F
      W X I O T C U E E O J E L
    S D A F G D H M Z U B Q W T S M P
  Q Y O R B K Y M B O R N E D L L F F O
 G C H K F A V F X A R E G A E S E G F F N
 V V P W X P A G M A N M E Z I Z M R N A W
D B O R M R F S G O Z E S V P S W A E A P Q C
Z M K U G O L B L R E H O E S O D H N L X T Q
Q I B Q M E C Q R W C E B H F A C B J R D W A I S
F I Z D K Q Y Z W Q B N D Y K L K Q D A C B H Y I
I E A F H F S J G Q M P C N V E Y I M G D N S N P
S O A U K B N C I O Y C N S S Y Y A Y V M T P W G L C
C K M W Q C R C J L T L P T L G S D E O U P R Z F N M
L D I V O P Y B H D L O T R R H T S S H B W Q C I R V
 I L X Y M K X E S K E D R V I U G O J A T T A B V
 B B W R P V P T C B I D S M S O E P S X R H B B O
 K Y Y W G Q T A H S Z T A P K R V S C Z T P R F K
 Y W L Q Q O N M Z P L J B I T U A T X B J E L
 I W C Y D U P I N K Y H I R G T G K F L F R R
  N E S N A J D R Z I Y U N J L N E O V G A
  R H I B B L T C N I M A C H A D O J H H O
    L I I E H T D U B G B B K W P Y L G G
      X V R V R N O E L D R I P O W Q F
      N D G M A Y T O J E Q R Y
        A V S U C O M D L
          T F N
```

PAGE 7

PAGE 8

PAGE 9
1. Blue Jays 2. 2
3. Willie 4. true 5. left-handed

PAGE 12

PAGE 13

```
                              ¹D
                          ²B A L L
              ³M           A
           ⁴H  I           M
           ⁵O U T F I E L D O
           M  T           N
           ⁶H E L M E T
           P
           L
           ⁷B A C K S T O P
           T
         ⁸B A S E
```

PAGES 14–15
Phillies: the Phillie Phanatic
Cardinals: Fredbird
Nationals: Screech
Red Sox: Wally the Green Monster
Mets: Mr. Met
Marlins: Billy the Marlin
Mariners: Mariner Moose
Astros: Orbit
Royals: Sluggerrr
Orioles: the Oriole Bird
Brewers: Bernie Brewer
Athletics: Stomper

PAGES 16-17

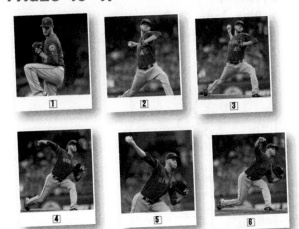

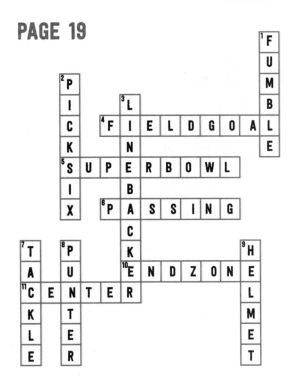

PAGES 22-23

PAGE 19

```
                                                    ¹F
                                                     U
           ²P              ³L                         M
            I               I                         B
            C          ⁴F I E L D G O A L
            K               N                         E
           ⁵S U P E R B O W L
            I               B
            X          ⁶P A S S I N G
                            C
           ⁷T    ⁸P         K               ⁹H
            A     U    ¹⁰E N D Z O N E       E
           ¹¹C E N T E R                     L
            K     T                          M
            L     E                          E
            E     R                          T
```

PAGES 20-21

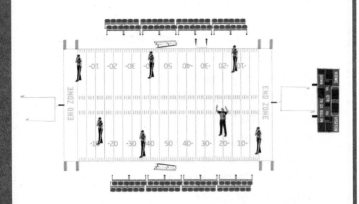

PAGE 26

PAGE 27

```
B E C K H A M
R       E
O       L
W       C A R R
N       E   Y
      B     A
G O R D O N       H
      A           I
S A N D E R S     L
      Y     M     T
            I     O
            T     N
      D A L T O N
            H
```

PAGE 28

1. Julio Jones 2. Khalil Mack 3. Matt Ryan
4. Tom Brady 5. Aaron Donald 6. Von Miller
7. Justin Tucker 8. Travis Kelce
9. Ezekiel Elliott
Extra word: **touchdown**
Bonus answers: pan, ant, the, her

PAGE 29

Antonio Brown, Calais Campbell,
Bobby Wagner, Casey Hayward,
T.Y. Hilton, Von Miller, Jay Ajayi,
Odell Beckham, Aaron Rodgers

PAGE 33

```
                 P X J
             F T E M V Y X U W
           W Y O H O P S J D V Y J Q
         F J J M F W N Q R P O E H H X F U
         X A X O J S B Z G A J Y H R W Z V G Q
       G N J T P P Y Y L L A W Y L T O T M F V J
       X P S J C A P D P L B N H E X F Z R G U N
     J Y A A S I U D U G U N U H Y G O D A L C G W
     Z P M Q B M L V D R U N E U P I V X T N D K G
   P B E S U G Y A A Z A N T E T O K O U N M P O G F
   U S F D X H E B Q T J E X H R W X J V N W H S T Q
   A V Y W H Z C V U I O X D I K N Z C N D R Y J D
   G I R A E S C Y J C P X T A L D K R C U L V X D O T K
   V T Z S U X R U W C N N X Y I R Z V R W R B T F M G
   A G C Z Z E Y S D R A N O E L I O I Q R M G K M Y V K
     Y X O H B E H C R Z I N A I B U R R Y K R X V I O
     A V C D N W Z U P O U T H O M A S I F R W K S O I
   K J N S I D D J P E D W D K E I L S H E P D R C Z
     K C Z I C C V R P J L M R R G T I N B L B I I
     W Y Q I B U Z U G W F W P O N W V X R T C F A
       H J L B P N F R E L T U B X M A F S D T J
       M P Y G Q O S X U Z O M H A R D E N Y N T
         W Q Z R E S P J S N O V P W F A L Y
           Y E Y T A R J D R J T I T G P G R
             N B Y J R O T H N K A V F
               X P L R H R A A H
                   L H K
```

PAGE 36

PAGE 38

Jimmy Butler, Kemba Walker, Kyrie Irving,
Kevin Durant, DeAndre Jordan,
James Harden, Gordon Hayward,
Paul George, Paul Millsap

PAGE 39

1. dribble 2. bank 3. rim 4. swish 5. lane
6. coach 7. arena 8. layup
Secret term: slam dunk

PAGE 40

dribble, bubble, hitter, tripping,
putter, full-court press,
ball, football

PAGE 41

Maya Moore

PAGE 42

Pictures 1 and 3 are the same.

PAGE 43

(Crossword answers)
1. GUARD
2. BUCKET
3. CURRY
4. FREE THROW
5. DRIBBLE
6. THE KING
7. KEY
8. GLASS
9. TIPOFF
10. SLAM DUNK
11. ASSIST

PAGE 44

Men's: UCLA, Kentucky, North Carolina,
Duke, Indiana
Women's: Connecticut, Tennessee,
USC, Louisiana Tech
Fill in the blank: Cut down the nets!

PAGE 45

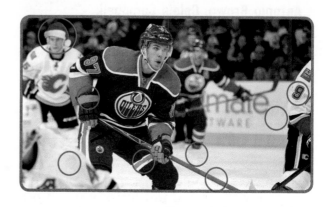

PAGE 47

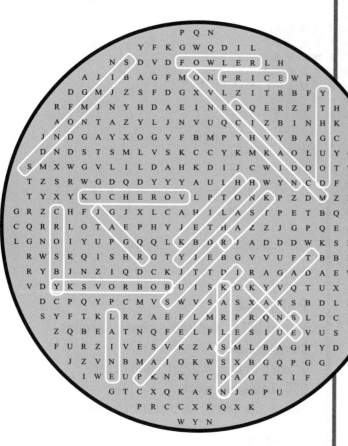

PAGE 57

PAGES 58–59

PAGE 49

Pictures 1 and 5 are the same.

PAGES 50–51

1. rink 2. Kings 3. saves 4. slap shot
5. Toews 6. sticks 7. Sidney 8. yes
9. skater

PAGE 61

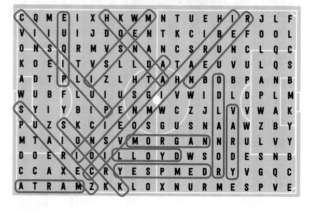

PAGE 62

1. 2, 45 2. up 3. b 4. save
5. foul 6. c 7. 7

PAGE 63
Dempsey scored the goal.

PAGE 65

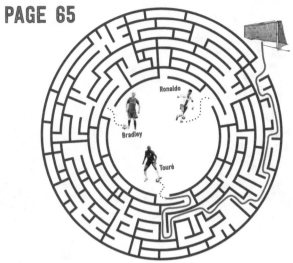

PAGE 68
Ramos: Spain, Rooney: England,
Neymar: Brazil, Ronaldo: Portugal,
Hernández: Mexico, Neuer: Germany
Secret answer: **goalie**

PAGE 69

					¹G					
					O					
		²C			A		³P			
⁴W	O	R	L	D	L	D	C	U	P	
		R			I		N			
⁵E	L	E	V	E	N		T			
		E								
⁶P	A	S	⁷S		⁸R	E	F	E	R	E	E
			P		K					
⁹T	H	R	O	W	I	N				
			T		C					
					¹⁰K	I	C	K		

PAGE 71

PAGES 72–73

PAGE 75

PAGE 77
1. stream   2. chaps   3. sight   4. hamper
5. bonus   6. opens   7. hoppin'
Answers: **Masters, British Open, U.S. Open,
PGA Championship**

PAGE 80

PAGE 81
trees

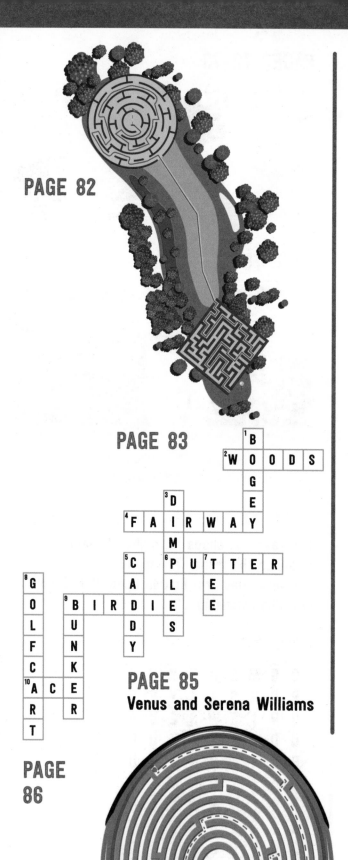

PAGE 82

PAGE 87

PAGE 83

Crossword puzzle answers:

1. B
2. WOODS
   BOGEY
3. D
4. FAIRWAY
   DIMPLES
5. CADDY
6. PUTTER
7. TEE
8. GOLFCART
9. BIRDIE
   BUNKER
10. ACE

PAGE 85
Venus and Serena Williams

PAGE 86

PAGE 90
Serena Williams, Rafael Nadal, Andy Murray, Angelique Kerber, Venus Williams, Roger Federer
Secret words: grand slam

PAGE 91

Crossword puzzle answers:

1. LOVE
2. LOB
3. DOUBLES
   DOUBLEFAULT
4. WIMBLEDON
5. BASELINE
6. GRAND SLAM
7. SERENA
8. ACE
9. RACKET

PAGE 93

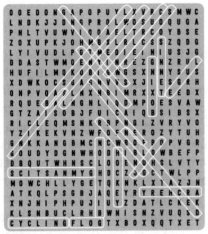

PAGE 95

Pictures 2 and 5 are the same.

PAGE 97

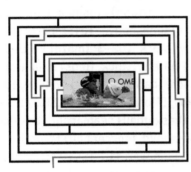

PAGE 100

1. Michael Phelps 2. Katie Ledecky
3. Simone Manuel 4. Anthony Ervin
5. Missy Franklin
2024 Summer Games: **Paris, France**

PAGE 101

Crossword answers:

1. TORCH
2. GREECE
3. WINTER
4. BRONZE
5. ANTHEM
6. RINGS
7. SWIMMING
8. BRAZIL
9. TRACK
10. SILVER
GYMNASTIC

PAGE 102

PAGE 105

1. Wall 2. ballpark 3. shallow 4. rally
5. mallard 6. curveball 7. Hall

PAGE 107

Trivia time: **Portland, Denver**

PAGES 114–115

PAGE 118

Crossword answers:

1. WATT
WILLIAM
2. PUJOLS
3. KANSAS
4. JOHNSON
5. BRADLEY
6. RODGERS
7. GARCIA
8. DURANT
9. VENN
10. MOORE

CREDITS

player) VasjaKoman; **2–3:** (Messi) FOTOPRESS, (Soccer ball) MauraHouston, (soccer player) bobvidler, (backboard) stephen_blair, (hockey player) duescreatius1, (soccer player) Smokeyjo, (pencil) Chud; **4–5:** (Babe Ruth) Photo Researchers, (Williams) staff, (Mantle) Louis Requena, (Gibson) Focus on Sport, (Maddux) Focus on Sport, (Griffey) Rob Tringali/Sportschrome, (scoreboard) stevezmina1, (McCutcheon) Jeff Zelevansky; **7:** (Utley) Mike Ehrmann, (deGrom, Stanton) Eliot j.Schechter, (Trout) Robert Binder, (Mauer) Tony Firriolo, (Miguel Cabrera) Mark Cunningham, (boys in rally caps) J Meric; **8–9:** (Bryant portrait and batting) Jamie Squire, (horse) John P Kelly, (top hat) Frank Mueller/EyeEm, (mole) Tim Oram, (baseball mitt) Erin Garvey, (butterfly) proxyminder, (kitten) Angiephotos, (periscope) Andrea Danti, (baseballl glove) JaimeAllen, (Wagner card) Chris Hondros; **10:** (baseball graphic) rambo182; **12–13:** (baseball player) Rob Tringali/ Sportschrome/Getty, (red flower) PM Images, (red glasses) Xose Casal Photography, (bow tie) Daniel Buitrago/EyeEm, (Sheriff's badge) Burazin, (cape) Paul Bradbury, (belt 1) Neil Lukas, (welliy) Gary Ombler/©Dorling Kindersley, (snowboot) objects. net; **14–15:** (Mr. Met) Slaven Vlasic, (background baseball pitch) David Madison, (baseball match images) R.Yeatts; **18–19:** (football icon) omergenc, (Thorpe) Hulton Archive, (Grange) MLB Photos, (Graham) Vic Stein, (Montana, Taylor) Focus on Sport, (Manning) Andy Lyons, (football figures) filo; **20–21:** (markers) Bruno Marsiaj, (referee) Kevin C. Cox, (upright) WesAbrams, (flag background) liangpv, (pitch graphic outline) appleuzr, (head referee) Icon Sportswire, (football stadium) Icon Sportswire; **22–23:** (pins for board) Dave King, (corkboard background) vuk8691, (game shots 1 & 2) Gregory Shamus, (game shots 3, 4, & 6) Icon Sportswire, (game shot celebration) Joe Robbins, (football) Filo; **24–25:** (footballer) Frederick Breedon, (Aaron Rodgers) Handout; **26–27:** (Tom Brady signing) Boston Globe, (Odell Beckham) Al Pereira, (football player) duescreatius1; **29:** (starburst with football) INDECCraft; **31:** (avocado) bubaone; **32–33:** (Robertson) Robert Abbott Sengstacke, (Russell) New York Daily News Archive, (Bird) Focus on Sport, (Johnson) Focus on Sport, (Leslie) Doug Pensinger, (Jordan) David Madison, (basketball players cartoon) duescreatius1; **36–37:** (Lebron James) J. Meric, (basketball graphic) omergenc, (Indiana pacers vs Cleveland Cavaliers) David Liam Kyle, (brown hat) Dave King, (dog) Life on white, (basketball) Gregor Schuster, (James Harden) Jennifer Pottheiser; **38–39:** (team line up) Bill Baptist, (basketball starburst, basketball in hoop) gyener, (Anthony Davis) Pool, basketball graphic (omergenc), (George) Joe Murphy; **40:** basketball cartoon (ScottTalent), (Westbrook portrait and action) Layne Murdoch, (Moore) Brian Babineau, (players at White house) Ned Dishman; **42:** (basketball silhouettes) VasjaKoman, (basketball match repeat) Bruce Bennett; **45:** (female basketball celebration) Ron Jenkins, (Statue of Liberty) Jewel Samad/AFP, (Washington) GraphicaArtis, (astronaut) QAI Publishing, (male basketball celebration) Jamie Schwaberow, (UFO) Aaron Foster, (shark) wildestanimal, (hockey player) Rich Lam, (football) AnthiaCumming; **46–47:** (Howe) Denis Brodeur, (Richard) Pictorial Parade, (Orr) Focus on Sport, (Lemieux) Denis Brodeur, (Grtezky, Roy) B Bennett; **48–49:** (Sergei B) Harry How, (Vezina, Weber) B. Bennett, (goalies) Jamie Sabau; **50–51:** (player 1) Joe Sargent, (player 2) Jonathan Daniel, (hockey player) Mark Murphy; **52:** (cartoon pencil) Chud; **54–55:** (players crash) Tony Duffy, (goal) Focus on Sport, (face off) Steve Powell, (players celebrating, handshake) Focus on Sport, (podium ceremony) Robert Riger; **56–57:** (santa hat) Lisa Noble Photography, (hockey match) Dan Riedlhuber, (catfish) larryrains; **58–59:** (red sweater) Patrick Mc Dermott, (black sweater) Jonathan Kozub, (orange & blue sweater) Andy Devlin, (star sweater) jamie Sabau, (Hawks sweater) Chas Agnello Dean, (penguin sweater) Joe Sargent, (yellow sweater) John Russell, (Toronto sweater) Mark Blinch; **60–61:** (Pele, Maradonna, Johan Cruyff) Staff, (Franz Beckenbauer) ullstein bild, (Lionel Messi, C Ronaldo) Denis Doyle, (soccer match) Matthew Ashton/AMA, (soccer ball repeat) MauraHouston; **62–63:** (tackle) Icon Sportswire, (scoreboard) Tom Pennington, (corner kick) Ira L. Black, (handball) Doug Pensinger, (referee) Alex Capparos, (soccer net) FrankRamspott, (Ronaldo)